950

D0373669

When Teens Stray

When Teens Stray

Parenting for the Long Haul

Dr. Scott Larson

with contributions from Peter Vanacore

SERVANT PUBLICATIONS
ANN ARBOR, MICHIGAN

Copyright 2002 by Dr. Scott Larson
All rights reserved.

Vine Books is an imprint of Servant Publications especially designed to serve
evangelical Christians.

Servant Publications—Mission Statement
We are dedicated to publishing books that spread the gospel of Jesus
Christ, help Christians to live in accordance with that gospel, promote
renewal in the church, and bear witness to Christian unity.

Unless otherwise noted, Scripture is quoted from the HOLY BIBLE, NEW
INTERNATIONAL VERSION. Other versions also quoted from: New Living
Translation (NLT), The Message, The Amplified Bible, The Living Bible (LB),
and King James Version (KJV).

To protect the privacy of the individuals whose stories are told in this book, the
names have been changed, although the stories are based on real events.

Published by Servant Publications
P.O. Box 8617
Ann Arbor, Michigan 48107

Cover design by Paz Design Group, Sisters, Oregon.

02 03 04 05 10 9 8 7 6 5 4 3 2 1

Printed in the United States of America
ISBN 1-56955-308-4

Library of Congress Cataloging-in-Publication Data

Larson, Scott, 1959-
    When teens stray : parenting for the long haul / Dr. Scott Larson; with con-
tributions from Peter Vanacore.
        p. cm.
    Includes bibliographical references.
    ISBN 1-56955-308-4 (alk. paper)
    1. Child rearing—Religious aspects—Christianity. 2. Parent and teenager—
Religious aspects—Christianity. 3. Christian teenagers—Religious life.
I. Vanacore, Peter. II. Title.
    BV4529 .L27 2002
    248.8'45—dc21

                                                                    2001008393

Contents

Acknowledgments

Thanks to Peter Vanacore, Karen Free, Dell Erwin, and Liz Heaney for the contributions, expertise, and tireless editing that have made this book so much better than it otherwise would have been. Thanks also to the many parents and teens I have interviewed over the past several years. Their courage to relive some of the pain from their past is what comprises the substance of this book.

Chapter One

Taking the Long View

The Lord has spoken: "I reared children and brought them up, but they have rebelled against me."

ISAIAH 1:2

When Carrie turned fourteen, she turned her parents' world upside down, too. Nothing they did seemed to work anymore. Nancy and Michael had been worried about their daughter for some time when a police call confirmed their worst nightmares.

Carrie had told her parents she was staying overnight at a friend's house, where she and Sara would be watching videos all night. But the police gave a different story. Neighbors had complained of loud music just after eleven o'clock. Further investigation revealed that twenty-six freshmen classmates were having a party while Sara's parents were gone for the weekend. Sara's older sister, who was supposedly left in charge, was spending the evening with her boyfriend.

"There were several bottles of hard liquor and numerous drugs confiscated tonight," reported the investigating officer. "Your daughter Carrie is in the bathroom vomiting. She's had a lot to drink. You'd better come down to the station right away."

A million questions raced through Nancy and Michael's heads as they headed out the door. *How had this happened? How could Carrie have lied to us like this? What else was going on over there? What if she's pregnant, too?* By the time they reached the station, both were seething with anger.

At first Nancy and Michael focused their anger on Carrie, but soon the conflict shifted from their daughter to each other. "If you hadn't been so selfish, wanting the prestige of a vice presidency in your company, this never would have happened," blamed Nancy. "You never once considered us in your decision to uproot and move us a thousand miles across the country. Did it ever occur to you that maybe this was a sacrifice not worth making?! Back in Youngstown, Carrie had good friends, loved the church youth group, and would never have been involved in something like this! I hope your new position has been worth it!"

Michael was equally infuriated. He had worked long and hard to provide the extra things he was now able to give his family. He hadn't heard Nancy complain the day they moved out of their cramped three-bedroom rambler in Ohio into a spacious four-bedroom colonial in a prestigious development of a wealthy suburb. He didn't like the extra hours he worked either, but he was doing it for his family. And if Nancy had worked harder to find a church with a good youth group instead of spending all her time buying new things for the house, he was sure this would not have happened.

Meanwhile, the incident was all over the local newspaper and the talk of the town. All the kids who'd been at the party were not only suspended from school, but also kicked out of any extracurricular activities they were involved in. Soccer had been the only positive thing Carrie had taken up since the move to Massachusetts, and now that was gone, too. Michael and Nancy felt embarrassed, isolated, and angry. But most of all they felt polarized and paralyzed, with no idea how to help their daughter or themselves.

No Simple Solutions

Wayward kids. They're always somebody else's—until yours approach the turbulent teenage years. When your child happens to be one who doesn't sail through adolescence so smoothly, suddenly all those easy answers you once clung to no longer seem so simple. You discover that your child's rebellion not only holds the potential to harm him or her, but every other member of your family as well. One child's rebellion can jeopardize the future of the entire family.

Scarcely a week goes by that my wife, Hanne, and I don't receive at least one phone call from parents like Michael and Nancy. Perhaps because our ministry deals with troubled teens, or because Hanne and I spent nine years taking kids from juvenile jails into our home, parents feel we can identify with their struggle. Sometimes we get heavily involved in the situations. Other times, we talk for only a few minutes over the telephone, passing on phone numbers of possible referral contacts.

While circumstances may differ, parents in pain ask similar questions:

"In what areas should I compromise?"

"Where do I stand firm?"

"Should I let the law deal with his illegal behavior or try to intervene to protect my son?"

"Do I insist that my daughter attend church as long as she's living in my home?"

"How can I trust my daughter when she has broken trust so many times in the past?"

"How do I know if it's time to remove my son from my home?"

"How can I be sure I'm doing the right thing?"

Questions like these don't come with easy answers or pre-scribed formulas. Yet parents are continually called upon to make quick decisions on such issues. Many of those decisions carry long-term consequences.

While doing research for this book, I met with scores of parents who have walked through the pain of parenting a rebellious child. I asked all of them what they had learned and what they would do differently if they could start over again. This book contains many of their stories, stories rich in the wisdom of God and life-changing lessons—often more so for the parents than for the children who caused them such pain. Many have regrets, but all have learned. Some have not yet experienced the return of their prodigals. Many others have.

Paul and Linda's story touches on a lesson that encompasses all the others: parenting for the long haul.

Parenting for the Long Haul

Paul and Linda were at their wits' end with their youngest son, Nick. "In the beginning, we were still protecting our own pride. But once neighbors see police cars in your driveway a few times, you're spending more time in your son's school than he is, and everyone in church knows of your son's prob-lems, your pride gets shattered pretty thoroughly," said Paul.

"After sitting around a table of school teachers, psychologists, and guidance counselors taking turns telling you why they don't want your son in their school any longer, you realize that you must let your pride go or it will destroy you, your marriage, and your child. It's at that point you must make a choice about how you're going to proceed. Nick was only fourteen years old, and it was clear to us that we had a few more difficult years ahead of us.

"That's when we finally made an appointment to see a counselor. We couldn't control whether we lost or kept our son, but we didn't want to lose our marriage as well. After hearing us pour out our hearts in that first session, the counselor gave these words of advice: 'Parent for the long haul.' It was the best counsel we could have received. It guided our decisions for the next decade, and does to this day."

Parenting for the long haul means parenting with the future in mind, trying to make each day's decisions with a mind toward five or ten years from now.

Another couple told me: "Parenting for the long haul has changed everything for us. I know that had we gone with the 'tough love' approach, I would not have a relationship with my son right now. At twenty-four he isn't living completely the way I would like, but I know that whenever I see him, he runs up to me, yells, 'Dad!' and throws his arms around me. For that, I'm eternally grateful."

Deciding to parent for the long haul gives you a framework in which to respond to questions like these:

Which battles am I going to fight, and on what hills am I willing to die?

What are the critical issues before us right now that threaten to jeopardize the safety of our child or our family if something isn't done?

What do I want my relationship with my child to be like in ten years, and what do I need to do now to ensure that?

How do I want my marriage to come through this, and what steps do I need to take to ensure that?

How will I deal with my own sense of pride and my natural inclination to "win at all costs"?

Jewels for the Journey

This book contains what I would tell every hurting parent if we could spend a few uninterrupted days together. It's sort of a road map for parents in pain. The territory that lies before you isn't uncharted, and insight from those who have gone before can make the journey a bit less paralyzing.

The next two chapters seek to dispel some of the myths that keep parents from effectively parenting for the long haul. From there we will explore several proactive principles that you can begin to apply immediately, principles to guide you as you practice parenting for the long haul. Don't try to incorporate them all at once—that would be too overwhelming. This book isn't meant to be exhaustive. If you need more indepth help for dealing with specific problems, I hope it gives you enough information to point you in the right direction.

Like most of the parents I interviewed, you may need to change in order to help your wayward child to change. I encourage you to pray—now, and as you read this book—that God would show you specifically how to approach your troublesome teen, and that he would soften your heart to make the changes you may need to make as well.

Are you ready to roll up your sleeves and uncover some of the lies and myths that may be hampering your effectiveness as a parent? If so, turn the page and let's begin the journey!

Chapter Two

Common Myths Parents Hold About Their Kids

A rebellious son is a grief to his father and a bitter blow to his mother.

PROVERBS 17:25, LB

One pastor told me, "I've counseled scores of people about what to do when their teenager wouldn't listen to them. I had all the right answers. But now that my own child is in serious rebellion, I'm finding that most of my theories just aren't working. I'm not sure if they're just not true or if my expectations are wrong. I'm not even sure whether it's my son who is the problem or if it's me. I feel stuck, and I can't see any light at the end of the tunnel."

Most of the advice we give and receive is not *all* bad. Usually there is at least an element of truth in it, and it may even have worked well for some other parent or for our other children. Most often, such advice is just incomplete, not taking into consideration the uniqueness of individual kids.

Still, we take those strands of advice and weave them into a rope that we believe will support us and our children. But there's nothing like a rebellious child to unravel the rope and leave us holding the frays. In the end, we realize that much of our foundation was built upon simplistic myths and faulty formulas.

In this chapter we'll explore some of the common myths parents hold about their children. If any of these myths reflect your own thoughts, ask God to help you shed it and replace it with truth.

Myth #1: If I do the "right" things, my children will turn out fine.

Keith and Marion couldn't understand why Cindy didn't respond to anything they tried: grounding her, removing privileges such as driving or going out with friends, talking to her. Nothing worked. Even though they both loved God passionately, their daughter had never been interested in spiritual things. Although they had raised her the same way they had raised her older brother Josh, the results couldn't have been more different.

Josh thrived in the youth group at church. Cindy refused to go. Josh begged his parents for a first job as a paperboy when he was ten years old. Cindy quit every job she had. Josh loved school and extracurricular sports. Cindy was expelled numerous times. She was certainly bright enough, but nothing seemed to engage her.

"What do we do with this girl? We've done all the right things. We took her to church from the time she was a baby. But none of it seems to have influenced her in the least," lamented her parents. Their home was frequently filled with yelling and fighting. At fifteen, Cindy had already run away several times.

Doing the "right thing" is very important, and in most cases, it does yield positive results. But not always. Sometimes, in spite of our best efforts, children do go astray. While we may be tempted to search for that one right method that can guarantee success in every case, it just doesn't exist. What's right for one child may fall miserably short for another. In parenting, one size doesn't fit all; we must prayerfully discern the "right" way for each child individually.

Yet many Christian parents cling to the myth, that if they do the right thing, they won't have problems with their children. They point to Proverbs 22:6: "Train up a child in the way he should go, and when he is old he will not turn from it." They take this verse to be a guarantee to all parents who rear a child in God's ways. If their child does rebel, these parents often respond in one of two ways. Some derive comfort from the assurance that their son or daughter will someday return to what they were taught as a child. Others see their child's waywardness as a personal failing in their ability to adequately train him or her.

Few biblical scholars, however, hold to the interpretation that Proverbs 22:6 offers a guarantee. Most agree that the book of Proverbs is written in the style of Hebrew wisdom literature, and that it reflects the observations of wise and godly people on daily living.[1] In fact, the definition of a proverb is "a short and pithy statement that captures a generalized observation about human life."[2] Yes, all Scripture is breathed by God and true, but proverbs aren't guarantees. They simply reflect what is generally true.

When Marion saw that their approach wasn't working, she decided to switch her game plan. "I'm going to make it my goal to really get to know Cindy; to try to understand her.

Right now, I don't even like her. I wish she were more like Josh. But she is still my daughter, and I know if I don't change something soon, I may lose her forever."

Rather than focusing on Cindy's smoking, music, and outrageous fashion preferences, Marion started by taking her daughter out for a Coke just to talk, with no agenda beyond getting to know her. At first, Cindy was suspicious, but over time she began to drop some of her defenses and revealed more of herself to her mother.

"I really like Cindy now," says Marion of her now twenty-one-year-old daughter. "She's a really neat girl. I wish she had a heart for God, but she doesn't. I keep praying for her, and some day I believe she will, but I can't make it happen.

"She still turns people's heads in public with her black clothes, wild hair, and body piercings. But I'm not as embarrassed as I used to be. And most of all, I'm glad I have my daughter. I almost lost her."

Keith and Marion had to learn to focus on who Cindy was as an individual rather than insisting that she be like her brother. They had to let go of their expectations in order to love her in the way that she needed to be loved. Accepting their daughter for who she was opened the door for Keith and Marion to have a real relationship with her. They still don't have any guarantee that Cindy will embrace Christianity or make the choices for her life that they want her to make, but they know that Cindy knows that they love and accept her—and they trust God with the rest.

Myth #2: My child just needs more discipline.
Problems emerge when parents gravitate to either of two poles in the area of discipline: some are far too permissive, others too strict. The balance is beautifully illustrated in the twenty-third Psalm, where David uses his background as a shepherd to express his understanding of God's love: "Your rod and your staff protect and comfort me" (Ps 23:4, NLT). The Middle Eastern shepherd used the staff as an instrument of love to draw individual sheep to himself. The rod was an extension of his right hand, a symbol of his strength and authority. It symbolized loving correction—not corporal punishment. Wise parents see discipline in the same way.

Recently, a Christian leader was telling me about his son, Peter. "All of our kids were raised going to church every Sunday morning, Sunday night, and Wednesday night. It was very important to me that we live by the Book. To me that meant swift and stern punishment. And it seemed to work fine for everyone—except Peter. I remember receiving a phone call from the police when he was ten years old, telling me he had been arrested for shoplifting a pornographic magazine. I gave him a walloping spanking when we got home. But I never talked with him about it. That was how I handled every situation.

"Years later I received a phone call from the president of a Christian college where I served on the board of trustees. He told me that Peter, who was a student there, had been found to be at the center of a crime ring on campus and was being kicked out of school. They required restitution and counseling before Peter would be allowed to return the following semester.

"One of the questions the counselor asked Peter was if he

had any family problems. He said, 'Yes, I don't really have a relationship with my dad.' That crushed me. I had thought I was one of the world's best fathers. I had chaired the deacons and most every other board at our church. I had even taught a popular Sunday school class on Christian parenting. And here was my son, saying he didn't have a relationship with me.

"But it did cause me to reassess, and eventually refocus, my entire life. I actually took a demotion, with a cut in pay at work, so that I could be home every evening with my family. I began talking with my kids about their recollections of me as a father. It took some convincing to get them to be honest because they didn't want to hurt me. They all said they could remember lots of spankings and lots of groundings. But none of them could recall a time where I sat down with them and explained why the thing they had done was wrong.

"Peter is a pastor today, and we have as close a relationship as any father and son could have. I'm so grateful for God's grace in bringing him back and for making our relationship so strong. But I wish I could live those days over again. I would have spent so much more time with him."

This father experienced the truth of an age-old formula: *Rules minus relationship equals rebellion.* God warns, "Fathers, do not embitter your children or they will become discouraged" (Col 3:21). Discipline alone is not the answer; your child needs first to know your love and acceptance.

Myth #3: If it worked for our other children, it should work for this one.

A pastor told me, "Our oldest and youngest have both turned out great. But my middle child, Ben, has been more than a handful. From the time he took his first steps, Ben was different. He always pushed the envelope. He did nothing the easy way.

"I should have noticed some of the early warning signs: how much he talked back to his mother and me; how he ran away for the first time at such an early age; how much he argued with us. Ben never backed down. He seemed to enjoy conflict and opposition.

"Once, when Ben was fifteen, my wife and I were away for the evening when we got a call from the police saying they had broken up a party at our house. Ben had passed out, and the house was completely trashed. The estimated damages came to more than $10,000.

"Shortly after that, I read a book on Type-T Personalities. Type-T stands for 'thrill seekers.' I realized that was Ben. He had always been motivated by the thrill of danger and adventure. Realizing that helped us understand him much better. I began to see that in the absence of positive ways to meet his need for adventure, Ben had engaged in thrill-seeking activities that were self-destructive.

"As I grew to understand my son better, I was able to help him by encouraging him to race motorcycles. The rules and regulations of racing made this sport much safer than other activities that Ben had been drawn to and it really helped to meet his need for adventure. I also asked him to consider starting a Bible study with me at a local detention center. Ben is so different than our other two children, but we have also come to see the great gift that is inherent in his personality."

Everyone has views on what successful kids look like. But every child is different, and as parents we need to recognize who our child is and adapt to his or her individual needs. As Proverbs 22:6 points out, we are to train children in the way *the child* should go. I like the way *The Amplified Bible* puts it: "in keeping with his individual gift or bent."

As parents, part of our responsibility is to discover and nurture our children's unique gifts and personality traits. Admittedly, this can be challenging. Some parents become paranoid at the least indication of a son who prefers more feminine activities like art, music, or acting to rough-and-tumble sports. They fear that such activities may lay the groundwork for homosexuality, though there is no evidence for such a link. As a result, parents might attempt to influence their son to be more athletic and discourage him from engaging in the arts, even though that may be what God had intended for him. We make a similar mistake when we try to force our daughters to be "nice little girls" when they're better suited to be hockey players or firefighters.

In addition, many parents struggle with the child who is strong-willed, assuming that he or she is just extremely rebellious. This was the case for my parents with one of my sisters, who has always been motivated by the challenge of tearing down obstacles in her path. In one instance, Susan was the first freshman in the history of our high school to be head majorette in the marching band. Halfway through the season, upset over an issue between the band instructor and one of the band members, she quit the squad as an act of protest. Ultimately, my parents had to learn to treat my sister very differently from the rest of us.

Going nose-to-nose with a strong-willed child in a power struggle only energizes the child. And in the end, a strong-willed child will most likely win anyway. It is difficult to outlast or break such a child—nor should you strive to. Cynthia Tobias, author of *You Can't Make Me!*, points out that strong-willed children have the capacity to change the world.[3] The question is, will it be for better or for worse? The answer often depends on what obstacles they're tearing down. Rather than try to break the spirit of a strong-willed child, far better to help redirect her energies. Send your child on a mission trip or get him involved in a service project. These tend to be very effective with strong-willed teens. Creating opportunities for them to rebel against the evils of poverty, racism, or injustice positions them to be a force for good in the world. If we don't steer them to larger and more appropriate battles, they'll tend to fight against all the things we want them to embrace.

Specialized circumstances and problems require specialized help. The issues surrounding rebellious children can be extremely complex. While we need to show consistency and fairness in how we treat our children, we also need wisdom from God as to how to respond to the unique personalities and issues that each of them possesses.

Myth #4: My child is causing trouble at school because he's ornery.

Many children who experience difficulties in school also possess some sort of learning disability or emotional or behavioral disorder. Such disabilities place a child at a disadvantage in school from the very beginning, the place where early socialization occurs—either successfully or not. When it is unsuccessful kids are much more quickly drawn to countercultural peers and lifestyles to gain acceptance and affirmation.

"When John entered middle school and was suddenly required to sit through six or seven lectures a day, he just couldn't do it," explained one father. "He is a very active, tactile, social learner—all of which his elementary school teachers recognized and were able to accommodate. But the cookie-cutter approach to education that he encountered in middle school set him up for immediate failure. I think that failure caused him to make a subconscious decision in the sixth grade to write off school. And he never reversed that decision."

The National Institute of Mental Health notes that while 15 percent, or one in seven, people in the United States have some learning disability, only 5 percent, or one in twenty, of all school-age children receive special education services for learning disabilities.[4] As parents, we must be sure that our child is not one of those who falls through the cracks and does not receive the special education services he or she needs.

Of the nearly four million school-age children who have learning disabilities, at least 20 percent have a type of disorder that leaves them unable to focus their attention.[5] Some have attention deficit disorder (ADD) and consequently appear to daydream excessively and are easily distracted. With boys in particular, the attention deficit is often accompanied by hyperactivity (ADHD). Such children act impulsively, run, jump, blurt out answers, and interrupt. Even when exhausted, they have trouble sitting still.

One father said this of his ADHD son: "In some ways it would have been easier if my son had a physical disability. Then the school makes wheelchair ramps and people cheer whenever small progress is made. But because his disability is invisible, they are only frustrated and fed up with him."

A growing number of researchers and educators are convinced that many children do not learn well in traditional teaching situations. Some believe that many children labeled learning disabled or ADD are simply children who are not taught in ways they can learn.

In his 1999 book, *Intelligence Reframed: Multiple Intelligences for the 21st Century*, Harvard psychologist Howard Gardner identifies nine different learning styles and preferences for how people learn. Yet most schools and even IQ tests focus only on two of these: linguistic and logical-mathematical intelligence. While traditional teaching methods work well for some children, they don't for all. If your child is having difficulty in school, consider using the assessment test in Appendix B to gain a better understanding of what his or her learning style is.

One mother said that she could tell within minutes of observing how a teacher taught whether or not her son would make it in that teacher's class. This mom worked hard to make sure her son had the most appropriate teachers for his learning style. She met with the principal and the teacher in an effort to help them better understand her son, and she became a partner with them in his education.

Another parent fought for a year to get his son into an alternative school. Finally, when he was about to be expelled for good, the school agreed to enroll him elsewhere. In a more individualized, structured program he made up three semesters of work in less than a year and graduated with flying colors.

Many children also struggle with emotional disorders that

make them susceptible to failure in school. One mother explained to me how her youngest had struggled greatly in school with both academics and low self-esteem. Later, as an adult, he was diagnosed with ADD, depression, and a slight mood disorder. "During those days we didn't hear much about the mental illnesses that may affect our children. It's hard for me not to cry when I think of all that Jeff went through in school.

"We took him to meet with a local pastor, who only further exacerbated the problem. His focus seemed to be on performance, seeing every failure as a sin and the result of not spending enough time in prayer and Scripture reading. His harsh, judgmental attitude was devastating to someone like Jeff, who could not achieve in the ways that others respected and expected.

"Today Jeff sees a therapist weekly, attends a weekly support group led by a therapist, and is making tremendous progress. I just wish I'd known then what I know now. It would have saved us all a great deal of pain."

Because of the many stresses placed upon today's teens, diagnoses of clinical depression are far more prevalent among teens than ever before. In fact, child psychiatrist David Fassler estimates that more than one in four of today's teens will experience a serious episode of depression by the age of eighteen, as opposed to a mere one in twenty in the 1960s.[6]

If you suspect your child may be suffering from a learning disability or emotional disorder, ask your school counselor to test your child. Such tests are usually offered without charge, and the information you glean can help direct you in knowing how to best help your child.

Myth #5: This child can no longer be trusted.
Parents who see their kids as untrustworthy in every area are making trust a black-and-white issue. It's not. Trust has varying degrees. You might trust your child in one area, but not in another. Trust is also incremental. It is earned, one step at a time.

When a child lies about one thing, a parent begins to wonder about everything. *What does he really do when he's out with his friends? Can I believe anything she says when it comes to why she missed her curfew or where she's going after school?*

Another cause of distrust stems from how trustworthy we as parents may have been as teens. That was certainly true for me. When Hanne and I had teenage boys living with us and they told me something, I couldn't help thinking about how I used those same lines to manipulate my own parents. Then I would get angry with them. Even if they were telling me the truth, I didn't trust them.

This, of course, can be very damaging to a child. Parents can push their children into delinquency when they always think the worst and don't believe *anything* they say. The child concludes, "Why should I even bother doing good? They don't believe me anyway." I had to pray for God to give me wisdom and discernment so that I didn't project my own past actions onto the children in my care.

But what if they do lie to you? It's best to be up-front and honest. I would say something like: "I want nothing more than to trust you—and I did trust you. I had no thought that you weren't doing what you said you were doing. But now trust has been eroded in this particular area. That doesn't mean I distrust everything about you, but I'm having a hard time trusting you in this area. I don't think you're a bad person, and I want to trust you again. It's just going to take some time for you to earn it back again. What things can we do to make that happen?"

Parents often ask me how much energy they should expend trying to find out what their kids are *really* up to every minute of the day. I don't think parents should ignore their suspicions, but neither should we go looking for reasons not to trust our kids. Far better to pray for your child and to ask God to alert you to the things you need to know.

For example, a couple of weeks after one of the boys from our home left for a Christian college, we found out that he had taken marijuana with him to sell just in case money got too tight. We were furious when we found out about it. I called him right away to confront him. But God had already gotten to him—without my help, if you can imagine that. As he attended chapel that first week of class, he was so convicted by the Holy Spirit that he went back to his room and flushed the drugs down the toilet.

I'm so glad we didn't find out what he was up to before he left for school, because I probably wouldn't have allowed him to go. As it turned out, he grew tremendously at that college, and from there went on to graduate school.

As parents, we are not to be naïve, but neither are we called to be Sherlock Holmes, always believing the worst and suspecting every little thing our children do.

Myth #6: Given enough time and space, my child will "grow out of it."

The belief that our children's problem behavior will disappear if we just wait long enough can be just as damaging as overreacting to their behavior. When I ask parents what they'd do differently if they had the chance, many say, "I would deal with issues as soon as they came to my attention and not ignore them, hoping they would go away. I discovered problems usually got worse, not better, when I didn't deal with them."

When we ignore a child's rebellious behavior, we are often acting irresponsibly, or we may just be in denial. Some parents are just too tired to deal with the problem. But kids can interpret a parent's passivity as not caring about them or as giving up on them.

Children know when they are doing wrong. When a parent lets a child get away with misbehavior, the child may wonder if he or she is lovable and capable of change. One boy in a juvenile jail told me, "I just wish someone would have cared enough to tell me 'No,' even when I fought with them about it." Another said, "I want someone to care when I do wrong."

When parents ignore the negative behavior of one child, it also puts the rest of the family in disarray. We have a responsibility to all of our children, giving them proper attention and protecting them from some of the dangerous effects of a rebellious sibling. Children need to know that their parents are able to weather the storms and dangers of the outer world, as well as stand up to their children's rages and unreasonable demands.

Interestingly, the dictionary defines *rebellion* as "the act of resisting or opposing the controls." Just as teens have a need to rebel, they also have a need for controls, or boundaries. Obviously, as kids grow older, the boundaries need to widen. But no matter where the boundaries are, kids will bounce off them and even overstep them a bit. Whenever boundaries are removed, kids tend to go crazy for a while. But eventually, most move back to where the boundaries were previously placed, as is illustrated below.

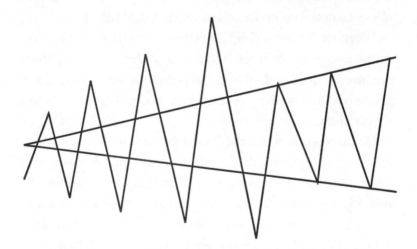

All kids need boundaries; they provide a much-needed sense of security. When they resist the boundaries, they are often testing them. This is healthy. Parents need to maintain boundaries—as long as they are healthy and appropriate for the child's age. I like the way Psalm 16:5-6 says it: "Lord, you have assigned me my portion and my cup; you have made my lot secure. The boundary lines have fallen for me in pleasant places; surely I have a delightful inheritance."

Myth #7: This child will never change.

Foster Cline and Jim Fay, authors of *Parenting Teens with Love & Logic*, say:

> The good news is that even if your child turns hard-core rebellious, if life was basically fine through age eleven you can take heart that things will turn out all right ... in the long run. The bad news is that the long run may be a *very* long run. Some of these teens don't get through those rebellious years until they're around 30 years old.[7]

If you are wondering if your child will ever change, take heart. Most kids do grow out of their rebellion. I recall reading a survey of people serving the Lord ten years *after* high school. Two common denominators emerged: First, they were raised in an environment where they saw authentic faith lived. Second, they rebelled against it for a time. Resistance to church is not the first step to atheism. When handled correctly, it is more likely to be a natural development in discipleship.[8]

Think back to the time when you were a teenager. On a scale of 1 to 10, where would you rate your own level of rebelliousness? My mother used to say to me, "I hope someday you have kids just like you." I have often wondered if opening our home to juvenile delinquents was somehow a fulfillment of her "curse"!

As radical changes take place in their bodies, adolescents go through tremendous internal pressure. We've all observed the difficulty some teens have in thinking logically. Interestingly, neuroscientists have shown that the last part of the brain to develop is the region that enables us to handle ambiguous information and make logical, coherent decisions. The prefrontal cortex, that part of the brain where sound judgments are formed, is not fully developed in most people until their early twenties.

Meanwhile, the limbic system, which generates raw emotions such as anger, is entering a stage of hyper-development—explaining at least in part how teens can be so moody, apparently making decisions based solely on emotions.[9]

Yes, things will change in the life of your teen. They will change in your life as well. And you may have much more power over changing the things that are really important than you realize. Keep reading!

Summary

Seven common myths parents hold about their kids:

- Myth #1: If I do the "right" things, my children will turn out fine.
- Myth #2: My child just needs more discipline.
- Myth #3: If it worked for our other children, it should work for this one.
- Myth #4: My child is causing trouble at school because he's ornery.
- Myth #5: This child can no longer be trusted.
- Myth #6: Given enough time and space, my child will "grow out of it."
- Myth #7: This child will never change.

Chapter Three

Common Myths Parents Hold About Parenting

They that observe lying vanities forsake their own mercy.
JONAH 2:8, KJV

One mother writes:

I arose early in the mornings to be alone with God. I fasted. I prayed. I even went so far as to go into his room and face down the myriad freakish posters and photos he had posted on his walls. I defied these people to try and steal my son's soul out from under me. I was soon to discover, however, that the problem with the all-out combat mode is that battle fatigue sets in before results. The more I prayed, fasted, and otherwise pulled out the stops in spiritual warfare, the more I expected measurable effects. When it became painfully evident that results were not part of this picture (at least at this point), the peaks of inspiration eventually were followed by troughs of dejection.[1]

At the root of parental disillusionment lies a host of unrealistic expectations. In the previous chapter we examined some of those held about our children, but even more destructive are those expectations we attach to ourselves as parents. The result is self-condemnation, which begins to erode our ability to trust God and to do what is best.

Here are a few of the most common myths parents believe about themselves.

Myth #1: If I just prayed more, my child would change.

Praying is one of the most powerful things a parent can do when it comes to a wayward child. We need to pray for our kids more often and with greater confidence, for God assures us that he hears our prayers and is delighted to answer. James 5:16 declares that prayer "is powerful and effective." But does it guarantee a quick turnaround in the heart of a rebellious teenager? Not necessarily.

God will never force anyone to surrender to him or turn from wickedness. He gives them every opportunity, yes. He often changes the circumstances around them. He even frustrates their wicked plans. But because he has granted his children free will, he will never violate their power to choose the way in which they live their lives.

Does that excuse parents from the responsibility of fervently praying for a struggling child? By no means. In fact, many parents greatly regret failing to pray daily for their kids, particularly those who later discover the extent to which their child was being influenced by destructive demonic forces. While we can't get God to control our child through prayer, in prayer we can do battle with those spiritual forces of darkness that are bent on derailing and devouring them (see Eph 6:12 and 1 Pt 5:8).

Myth #2: I can get my child to change if I don't give up.

The belief that we have the power to change our children is a hard myth to relinquish. Generally we know what's best for our children and want to spare them unnecessary pain and suffering. But we can never control another person, not even our own child. Attempts to do so through guilt or manipulation often backfire. As a general rule, the more guilty we make our children feel, the worse they tend to behave, even when they want to do otherwise. In our attempts to rescue them, we can actually prolong the process.

Dennis had lived with us for three months when he came home one night completely inebriated. Rather than dealing with him in that state, we decided to wait until morning. When Hanne and I spoke to him, his response was, "You just don't understand. I've been an alcoholic since I was twelve years old. My mother's an alcoholic. My father's an alcoholic. My grandparents are alcoholics. It's all I'll ever be."

"But Dennis," we said, "You're a new person now. God has made you *new*. The old you is gone."

"No. I've tried changing before. I knew it was just a matter of time before I'd fall right back into the same old stuff. I'm surprised I lasted this long."

"But we want to help you, Dennis. We'll talk with you every day about it. We'll hold you accountable ..."

"You don't know me," he argued. "This is just who I am."

Finally it dawned on us. We were convinced that Dennis could change. We were willing to do whatever it took. But was he?

Then Hanne asked him, "Dennis, do you want to change?"

"I already told you. I'm an alcoholic. My mother's an alcoholic ..."

"But, Dennis, what about you? Do you want to change?" Hanne interrupted.

There was a long silence. "No. No, I guess not," he finally sighed.

We couldn't do anything to help Dennis unless he himself wanted to change. As someone once said, "Until the *pain of staying the same* becomes greater than the *pain of changing,* nobody will choose change." Dennis ended up leaving our home shortly after this conversation, and went on to experience some very difficult times. Eventually he concluded that his life was not heading in a direction he wanted to go, and that he needed to make some drastic changes. While we had provided him with many of the tools for change, it wasn't until he had reached bottom that he possessed the most important tool: a desire to change.

Until your child wants to change, all you can do is pray and make the necessary adjustments to protect yourself, your child, and the rest of the family.

The father of the Prodigal Son let his son go, and God the Father does the same with us. He refuses to coerce, even though he could. There is a limit even to his pleading. He does not block the doorway as we try to leave him, flooding us with a thousand arguments. Nor does he pursue us, pestering us with, "I told you so." He gives us the full dignity of choice. There is wisdom as well as justice in what he fails to do; there is nothing like a belly full of husks to teach a man that he's a fool.[2]

Sometimes we *have* to let go before we can get a wayward

child back. But remember, God doesn't give up on any of us. He is the great Pursuer and is far better equipped to bring your child back than you are. Allow him to uniquely comfort and assure you in those moments when you most need it.

One mother explained how God met her one Sunday morning. "My sixteen-year-old daughter, Jessica, ran away from home just a week before Christmas and was gone for six months. I was in so much pain during that time. At the close of a church service, our pastor felt led to call any of those in the congregation who were feeling anxiety over difficult family situations to come forward for prayer. I was the first to go down. After I told him some of what was going on, he said, 'Sounds like she's working on a future testimony.' That stuck with me for a long time. It gave me a longer term perspective on both God's faithfulness and on the fact that age sixteen wasn't the end of the road for Jessica."

Myth #3: If "such and such" happens, I won't make it.
Fear kicks in when parents begin thinking about all the disasters that could befall their wayward child. "Lord, if this happens, I'll go crazy. I just couldn't take it!" If, and when, "it" does happen, we usually don't go crazy. But fear can cause us to respond in ways that inflict more harm than good.

Fear can paralyze us and keep us from demanding appropriate behavior from our children when we're afraid they might
- run away
- drop out of school
- lose their job
- speak negatively about us to significant others

- report us to child welfare for child abuse
- turn further away from us and toward the wrong crowd
- get deeper into drugs and/or alcohol abuse
- get pregnant or impregnate someone else.[3]

When we allow our fear of what our children might do to control our response to them, our ability to love them as God commands us to is limited. To the degree our actions are motivated by self-protection, we are unable to focus on what's really best for our child. Let me illustrate.

Shawn lived with us for about a year after he was released from a juvenile jail. He was doing fairly well until his father began intervening. His dad loved Shawn dearly, but carried tremendous guilt for years of abandoning his son for alcohol. Now sober, he was trying to make up for lost time. Shawn, like most kids, knew how to play his dad with perfect precision. Because Shawn's father feared that telling his son "no" would make his son feel like he was letting him down again, he fell into the trap of enabling Shawn's destructive behavior.

Soon after moving in with us, Shawn got two speeding tickets. The second one carried a fine of $300, and the court was threatening to take away his license if he didn't pay. Shawn called his dad, who bailed him out. A few months later, when Shawn got into an accident and didn't have the $500 deductible to get his car fixed, his dad paid for that as well. As a result, Shawn was never forced to take responsibility for his actions. Because he was never allowed to suffer the painful consequences for his actions, he missed the opportunity of learning from his mistakes.

Today Shawn is twenty-four, and his dad is still bailing him out of this and that. As a result, Shawn is not much further along in his maturity than he was when he lived with us at age seventeen.

How can you tell if you are enabling your child rather than helping him or her? Check the motives behind your actions. When that's hard to sort out, seek the perspective of a trusted friend, pastor, or counselor.

While Shawn's father gave in to his son's demands out of guilt and fear, other parents may become paralyzed by panic, unable to sleep at night as their imaginations run wild. Matthew 6:25 tells us not to worry about tomorrow. Why? Because our heavenly Father knows what we need and will care for us. He also promises in 1 Corinthians 10:13 that he will not allow us to be tested beyond what we can bear.

Philippians 4:6-7 admonishes us to "not be anxious about anything, but in everything, by prayer and petition, with thanksgiving, present your requests to God," promising that "the peace of God, which transcends all understanding, will guard your hearts and your minds in Christ Jesus."

One mother I know experienced a breakthrough when she was convicted that overanxiety was a sin that she needed to repent of. When she did, she started focusing on God's truths rather than the devil's "what ifs."

If you struggle with anxiety and distress over your teen, make a decision to put your prayers and energy into thinking about how to best parent him or her for the long haul rather than dwelling on what might go wrong.

If you feel unable to control your anxiety, you're in good company. As one mother confessed, "I prayed and prayed, claiming God's peace over my anxiety, but the fears for my children still would not subside." She found it helpful to write down all of those fears that related to her children, then share it with a trusted friend who would be faithful to pray for her as well as her children.

As you pray, ask God to reveal the source of your anxieties. Such fears are often rooted in past experiences where we have felt neglected or abandoned. Other times, they are patterns that have been passed down to us for generations. But God wants to free us from worry. He has not given us a spirit of fear; but one rooted in power, and love, and a sound mind (see 2 Tm 1:7). God will often use difficulties with our children to shed light on our own areas of pain and brokenness, and in the process bring us to a place of healing and wholeness.

Myth #4: My home should be a haven of peace.
While understandable, the expectation that our homes should always be peaceful simply isn't realistic. If we expect home to be a respite from the struggles of the day, we will be in for great disappointment from time to time.

Christian parents are particularly prone to this fantasy expectation, especially if we've sat through one of a myriad of Christian family seminars and workshops or read some of the Christian self-help books designed to explain the biblical view of family life. In the end, it's easy to conclude that if Dad would just assume his place as the head of the household, and Mom would be submissive, and all the kids would just remember to respect Mom and Dad, family life would be like the Hallmark cards or Taster's Choice ads.[4] Such an ideal only contributes further to Mom and Dad's emotional distress and shame by somehow painting a picture of what godly families "ought" to be.

Family therapists Jack and Judith Balswick point out that just as our kids reach adolescence, we parents are often entering midlife. These two developmental stages both bring a tremendous amount of stress. Thus, the stress of adolescence does not merely add to parental midlife stress, it multiplies it. But so is the effect of a parental midlife strain upon the adolescent.[5] The two must be seen as interactive. Whenever more than one family member is experiencing great personal anxiety, the potential for conflict in the family increases exponentially.

Parents of rebellious children often feel an additional sense of failure and inadequacy. Many feel isolated as they attempt to protect themselves or their children from the criticism or gossip of others. These stressors can polarize couples at the very time they most need to draw strength from one another.

Certainly it is not wrong to want our homes to be places of peace and rest, but to expect teenage children to make significant contributions toward that end is a bit unrealistic. It is *our* responsibility as parents to ensure that home is a place of refuge where our children feel safe and secure. But hang on. Chances are, your turbulent child today will be back as a contributing peacemaker a few years down the road.

Myth #5: If I weren't a single parent, my child wouldn't have these problems.

The belief that single parenthood automatically creates negative behavior in children assumes that parents are solely responsible for all their children's problems. But countless families have proven this isn't so. Scores of kids raised in single-parent homes turn out exceptionally well; just as many children raised in two-parent families exhibit significant problems.

Don't fool yourself into thinking that you wouldn't be having problems if you were married. It's not true. Even more, it does nothing to restore your relationship with your child.

Having said that, let me add that single parents do face some unique challenges. One single mother recently told me: "Jeff has always been a great kid. That is, until this year, when he turned sixteen. Now it seems anger is erupting all over him. For one thing, his father is back in his life again. Trying to make up for lost time, my ex-husband promised Jeff a car as soon as he got his license. So now, of course, Jeff hounds me nonstop for his license. I told him I don't have the money for driver's ed right now, and I don't even think he's ready for it yet. He just started a part-time job and is already having problems trying to juggle that with schoolwork. I've refrained from expressing my serious doubts that his father will actually follow through on this promise."

It's common for kids to play one parent off the other, and all the more when the parents are divorced. If you find yourself in such a situation, for your child's sake, don't bad-mouth the other parent. As poorly as the estranged or absent parent may have behaved, children need both parents as much as possible. To force a child into the awkward role of taking sides only exacerbates the pain and inevitably comes back to haunt you in the long run.

Another mother told me: "My sixteen-year-old daughter suddenly wants a relationship with her father. She and I have always been the closest of friends. She's been my life. But now it's like I'm her worst enemy. It all started when she wanted to live with her father for the summer, which I had serious reservations about. Now she calls me and says she'd like to live with him for her last two years of high school! What have I done to deserve this? I sacrificed an education and a career for her, and now here I sit with my waitress job and nothing."

This mother needs her daughter as much or more than her daughter needs her. While it's understandable, it's not healthy. As parents, we are entrusted with the care and nurturance of our children, but then we're required to release them. An old proverb I like a lot says, "We have two great gifts we can give to our children. One is roots. The other is wings."

Many children in single-parent homes express a desire to live with the other parent when they reach their teenage years—even if they never have before. (Adopted children will often become consumed with wanting to locate their biological parents as they enter adolescence.) This desire has much more to do with their maturity and development than it does with how they feel about you. Teens need to individuate from their parents and find their own identity. As parents, we need to encourage and support them in this process; otherwise, we set ourselves up to be the ones pushed out of their lives.

Single-parent households comprise nearly half the homes in America.[6] Yet the roles played by both a father and a mother in a child's life remain essential for kids to develop into healthy adults. While nobody can replace a missing parent, God can raise up men or women who can be significant role models for your child. Sometimes it's a coach or youth worker, other times a relative.

The apostle Paul played this powerful role in the lives of several people. To a band of people in Corinth he said, "Even though you have ten thousand guardians in Christ, you do not have many fathers, for in Christ Jesus I became your father through the gospel" (1 Cor 4:15). He was a father figure to Timothy (1 Tm 1:2), Titus (Ti 1:4), and Onesimus (Phlm 1:10) as well. Even teens living with both parents can benefit from such an adult in their lives. But single parents in particular should pray for someone like this to influence their child, and consider doing the same for someone elses.

Myth #6: My children are a direct reflection on me.
The belief that our children's behavior directly reflects our own character is probably the most common myth that parents hold about parenting. When others observe our child's negative behavior, it's easy to imagine they're critiquing our ability—or inability—to "control our own household." The extent to which we will go to save face or protect our pride knows no end.

I have spoken with countless Christian leaders who wonder if their child's rebellion disqualifies them from engaging in fruitful ministry. They cite Titus 1:6: "An elder must be blameless ... a man whose children believe and are not open to the charge of being wild and disobedient." Yet such an across-the-board interpretation would eliminate God himself from ministry. Consider how his first two children, Adam and Eve, turned out, not to mention that his first grandchild became a murderer!

When God granted freedom of choice to his children, he also relinquished some of the control he had over the rest of his creation—and at the same time opened himself up to deep pain. Hear it expressed in his words in Isaiah 1:2: "The children I raised and cared for have turned against me" (LB). Many Christians ignore such realities, however, choosing instead to use scriptural principles and proverbs as a means to arrive at simplistic solutions. For example, the declaration in Exodus 20:5 that "the sins of the fathers are visited to the third and fourth generation" was never intended to place blame upon parents when their children go astray, as if God were punishing parents for their own sins. In the same way, the declaration in verse 6 that "mercy is shown to thousands of generations to those who love me and keep my commandments" is no guarantee that our children and grandchildren will make good choices for their lives just because of our faithfulness.

So what is this passage saying? The Hebrew word translated *visit* in verse 5 is the same term that was used for taking a census or head count. In other words, when a parent sins and rebels against God, his or her offspring *may* share some of those same tendencies—but not always.

While the majority of troubled kids do come from dysfunctional homes, there's no guarantee that good parenting will automatically produce good children. The reality is, if you have three or more children there's a good chance that one of them will exhibit serious signs of rebellion in the teenage years.

In Ezekiel 18, God takes great pains to warn his people about the danger of misusing Scripture—apparently a problem that was just as common back then as it is today. Notice what the prophet says:

What do you people mean by quoting this proverb about the land of Israel: "The fathers eat sour grapes, and the children's teeth are set on edge"? As surely as I live, declares the Sovereign Lord, you will no longer quote this proverb in Israel. For every living soul belongs to me, the father as well as the son—both alike belong to me. The soul who sins is the one who will die.

EZEKIEL 18:2-4

The proverb Ezekiel is referring to comes from Job 21:19, where Job's friends used it to say that Job's shortcomings as a father were the source of his problems.

Ezekiel 18 exposes the error inherent in this line of reasoning, culminating in verse 20: "The son will not share the guilt of the father, nor will the father share the guilt of the son. The righteousness of the righteous man will be credited to him, and the wickedness of the wicked will be charged against him."

At the conclusion of the chapter, God admonishes both parent and child, saying: "I will judge you, each one according to his ways, declares the Sovereign Lord. Repent! Turn away from all your offences; then sin will not be your downfall. Rid yourselves of all the offences you have committed, and get a new heart and a new spirit.... For I take no pleasure in the death of anyone, declares the Sovereign Lord. Repent and live!" (Ez 18:30-32).

We all make mistakes. Some of those mistakes are terrible. But rather than continually punishing ourselves, we need to openly confess those mistakes to our children. We need to ask for their forgiveness and start over, doing what is right. As Ezekiel points out, there's not much value in stewing over sour grapes!

Much as we'd like to change the course of our children's lives, they are ultimately responsible for their own actions, just as we are responsible for ours. When we step in—often for the sake of preserving our own reputation—we can sometimes short-circuit what God is able to do in their lives, a process that may require them hitting bottom.

If you take away one truth from the last two chapters, let it be this: *You cannot control another human being, even if that human being is your own child.* You may discipline and teach; you may train; you may point out the right course; you may shape behavior patterns; you may reason; you may plead and you may pray. But you cannot control. As a parent, you can only assume responsibility for those things that you can change or control, the very issues that are the substance of the remainder of this book. The rest you must entrust to God.

Now, let's turn our focus to those things that you *can* do.

Summary

Six common myths parents hold about themselves:

- Myth #1: If I just prayed more, my child would change.
- Myth #2: I can get my child to change if I don't give up.
- Myth #3: If "such and such" happens, I won't make it.
- Myth #4: My home should be a haven of peace.
- Myth #5: If I weren't a single parent, my child wouldn't have these problems.
- Myth #6: My children are a direct reflection on me.

Chapter Four

Protecting Your Marriage and Family

I prayed for this child, and the Lord has granted me what I asked of him. So now I give him to the Lord. For his whole life he will be given over to the Lord.

1 SAMUEL 1:27-28

A rebellious child places more stress on a family than almost anything else. In fact, disagreements and conflicts that result from the stress of parenting such a child are one of the leading causes of divorce.

I have a good friend on staff at a large parachurch ministry who went through a terrible time with his son. He ended up losing his wife, his ministry position, and his family.

Another friend whose son rebelled was more fortunate. "By God's grace my wife and I have stayed together, and for the most part, united through it," he told me. "But Ryan's rebellion came at a particularly hard time for us both, as my wife was also going through menopause. Because she already felt traumatized in general, I felt like I couldn't share all the ugly, gory details of our teen's behavior with her, and I felt very alone."

What can you do to ensure that you, your marriage, your family, and your relationship with your wayward child remain intact?

To help answer that question, I conducted multiple interviews with parents whose adolescents had seriously rebelled. I asked each of them what they would do differently if they could. The eight principles that appear in this chapter and the next arose from their responses.

Invest in Your Marriage

Many of the couples I talked with said that the most important thing they believed they could do for themselves and their kids was to invest in their marriage—especially during times of stress, as that's when their marriage needed help the most.

What are some things you can do to invest in your marriage while parenting a wayward child?

Practice healthy communication skills.
When Hanne and I ran our home for boys, our relationship often became polarized. I wanted to kick kids out; Hanne wanted them to stay. I was more inclined to punish; Hanne tended toward leniency. As a result, we were unable to discuss anything pertaining to the home without causing major dissension in our relationship. We both felt extremely alone at the times when we needed each other more than ever. After the first few boys, we resolved never to allow anything to polarize us like that again. It was a lesson we learned the hard way.

How does one undo such deep-seated patterns of unhealthy communication? For starters, Hanne and I had to establish new rules of engagement. For example, when Hanne wanted to discuss something that she knew might surface a negative reaction in me, she would warn me first, assuring me she wasn't attacking me; she just needed to talk about it. I would then commit to listening to her and reflecting back what I heard her saying, void of any personal commentary. If my interpretation was consistent with what she was saying, I would then proceed to tell Hanne how her viewpoint made me feel—not what I thought, but how I felt (an important, but difficult, distinction for most men). She in turn would reflect back to me what I had said, and then express how that made *her* feel.

After this sometimes lengthy process, we would together decide on a course of action if one was needed. While such rules may seem rather rigid to some, they often served to keep our relationship off the battlefield.

Show each other affection.

Your spouse needs to know that you love and value him or her—particularly when your family is undergoing major stress. Now more than ever is the time to be affectionate and loving toward each other, both in private and in front of your kids. This not only bolsters your marriage relationship, it's good for your kids. Children need to see healthy affection and love between their parents. It gives them an increased sense of security as few other things do. Parents can get away with many mistakes if their children see them as a solid, loving alliance.

Ask for help if your marriage is suffering.

An outside counselor can help you deal with issues that may be threatening your marriage relationship. A counselor can hold you accountable to keep talking and communicating in ways that are healthy and helpful, as well as provide you with practical ideas about how to deal with your rebellious child.

Without outside help, it's easy to become entrenched in destructive patterns in your marriage that will remain even after the crisis with your child has passed.

Schedule a weekly date night.

A weekly night out is a necessary time to focus on each other and to nurture your relationship. You may not feel like you have the time or the energy to do this, but neglecting your own relationship as husband and wife is deadly. Avoid discussing the all-too-familiar topic of your child and his or her behavior while you are out together. This will pay big dividends, both in the present and in the years to come.

Divide up the parenting responsibilities according to each one's strengths and personalities.

Sit down with your spouse and identify each of your strengths as well as those parenting tasks that are best suited to each of you. This division of labor will conserve your energy and better prepare you to respond in a crisis.

One father told me, "My wife dealt with the side of Mark that thinks there'll never be a tomorrow. That part of him that never saves a receipt, school assignment, or any written instructions. She is very organized and does well with details. I, on the other hand, am better at dealing with crises. Consequently, I dealt with the schools, employers, and police.

"One of our more stressful times was when Mark was arrested the night before his sister's wedding. The police called, requesting that he stay in jail until his court appearance Monday morning. I explained that it was his sister's wedding the following night and how much it would mean to his sister if he could stand up in the wedding. I promised that I would deliver Mark into their custody first thing Monday morning. They agreed.

"Because we had already agreed on what each of us would handle as parents, Sue was able to focus on caring for our daughter and all the details of the wedding. Though it was difficult, we each knew our roles and the weekend turned out remarkably well."

Present a United Front to Your Child

It can be difficult for parents to agree on a course of action, but even if you are divorced from the other parent, it's critical for your child. His well-being depends on your unity. In fact, the welfare of children rests more on parental unity than on any child-rearing technique either parent may possess.

To present a united front, focus on these key areas:

Agree on a method of discipline.

As a general rule, the more irresponsible the teen, the more critical it is for parents to agree on the type of discipline they use. Argue, disagree, and debate all you need in private before coming to a decision, but never in front of your child. Defiant children are masters at locating and pitting one parent against the other in every area where parents are not unified.

Each parent brings his or her own perspective to this topic, but many of the parents I talked with told me they were less likely to be polarized about the *method* of discipline when they were able to agree upon the primary *goal* of discipline. For example, if one of your agreed-upon goals is parenting for the long haul, you will want to choose a method of discipline that helps preserve your relationship with your child and that will also build your child's character.

This process of coming to agreement ahead of time may be difficult in the beginning, but it gets easier with each decision made, and fewer decisions have to be overturned later. In those areas that remain confusing, seek counsel from more experienced, godly parents who have weathered their own share of tough times with their teens.

Agree about when you will step in to provide financial help.
The decision to give money was always a tough one for us. We had guys who had left our home, got into trouble, and needed money to post bail or pay speeding fines so they could keep their driver's licenses and not lose their jobs. In every case, we felt that no matter what we did we would come out the loser. If we didn't lend them the money, they would take it as an expression of rejection. If we did, we rarely got the money back. Even worse, our relationship was strained because of the guilt and shame the teen felt for not paying us back.

Hanne and I could have benefited from having a standard to fall back on when such situations arose. I like what one couple I interviewed decided to do.

"We would stand with our son, Jamie, whenever we sensed he was trying to make significant improvements. We would help him financially with things like books for schooling or suits for a new job when he needed them. But one of our hardest decisions came when he called and said, 'You know that $250 you sent me? I lost it in a pool game. Not only that, but I owe another $250, and the guy says if I don't pay him back right away he's going to hurt me real bad.'

"'Oh come on, Jamie, he's going to beat you up for $250?' I challenged him.

"'Dad, believe me, that's the least of what he'll do.'

"It was so hard to say, 'You know we'll always be there to help you as long as you're making positive choices, but we don't have $250 to pay off your gambling debts.' And Jamie did get beaten up. It was hard to watch, but I think we did the right thing. It was a painful lesson he needed to learn in a painful way."

Agree to speak to your spouse before making decisions on predetermined issues.

Make a list of the things you need to discuss with your spouse before giving your child permission to do them. This can save you a lot of energy. For example, if your son says, "I'm going to a party at Kevin's," but as parents you've agreed he needs both parents' approval to attend a party, tell him you have to talk it over with your spouse. This buys you some time so that you won't be caught off guard and gives you the benefit of another perspective.

When you follow this guideline, you'll be far less likely to have to reverse a decision, and you'll experience less anxiety over your decisions. Parents who are able to apply this strategy for addressing conflicts with their teens generally find their homes to be much more peaceful and experience less of the pitting of one parent against the other.

Discussing decisions with an ex-spouse, of course, can be more challenging. Teens can play one parent against the other more easily when they're apart, especially if the parents have a poor relationship. If this is your situation, you might try to bring a third party in to help negotiate a discussion with the other parent. Many counseling agencies have trained family mediation specialists who can provide a neutral platform to work on a strategy that works for both sides.

Build a Support Network

When Rob and Cindy were struggling with their son, Bobby, their small group at church became a lifeline for them. Cindy told me: "Though no one said it directly, we felt condemned by many people in our church. And after awhile, people seemed to get burned out from hearing the same sorts of responses to their inquiries of, 'How's Bobby doing?' Consequently, we started attending one of the megachurches in our area for anonymity, so we wouldn't have to keep reporting the same or worse situations when people said they were praying and wanted to know the results. We felt the same way with Christians with whom we worked, and those we saw every day.

"We couldn't turn to family for help, either, because we didn't want them to think negatively about Bobby. If he did eventually turn his life around, we didn't want them to be tempted to hold against him all that he had done in the past. It really was our small group that held us together. The night we had to have Bobby hospitalized because of an overdose, we called our friends in despair. Though it was very late, they came right over."

Most parents of wayward kids minimize the pain and try to solve the problem themselves. We don't want others to know about our problems because we're embarrassed or ashamed. We don't want others to look at us or our child in a negative light.

But parents who have been the most successful in parenting a troubled teen say that a support network was critical to their survival. One pastor told me: "Our first two sons were extremely rebellious and often in trouble. But we decided not to hide it from people in the church. We asked for prayer many, many times. And as long as we were open, people loved and supported us tremendously, and we had many opportunities to help others who were hurting with their children as well."

While every situation is different, God has made us in such a way that simply sharing our burden with another person serves to lighten the load. I would go even a step further: In every case I have observed where people have come successfully through a personal or family crisis, they give credit to a family member or close friend who played a key role in helping them get through it.

Here are some guidelines for building a support network:

Solicit the help of some trustworthy confidants.

Proverbs 17:17 says, "A friend loves at all times, and a brother is born for adversity." We desperately need friends in times of adversity to share our pain, but it's essential that we use wisdom in selecting those we rely upon for in-depth support and counsel.

Enlist the help of people who
- aren't easily shocked and can accept honest feelings
- aren't uncomfortable or embarrassed by tears
- will listen without giving unsolicited advice
- are faithful to commitments and promises
- can be trusted to not gossip and betray confidences
- know how to be helpful in practical matters
- can help bring God's perspective to the situation
- will pray with you and for you
- are familiar with the stages of grief and may have experienced brokenness themselves
- do not spiritualize and try to force-feed you theology and Scripture.[1]

Meet with your chosen confidants regularly.
Once you find the right persons to help you process some of your pain, meet with them regularly. By meeting with a smaller network of people consistently, you're more likely to receive genuine feedback on how you're doing from week to week. Just knowing that others are standing with you, praying when you no longer have the strength or the faith to do so, can make all the difference.

Be prepared with respectful responses to not-so-respectful questions or comments.
There is never a shortage of people who know of a similar case and are ready to give suggestions about what you should do. Often, however, their advice is contrary to your selected plan or what you have determined with your counselor or support team. At times, dealing with unhelpful advisors can be more

stressful than the crisis itself. (Job had the same problem with his friends.)

Rather than getting angry, try one of these respectful responses to some of the not-so-respectful questions and comments you'll likely receive:

When they say, "I didn't know your son was on drugs. How come you never told me?" *you can say,* "Some things are not easy to talk about. Perhaps we can discuss it at another time."

When they say, "You and your wife are such nice people. I can't believe your daughter is actually an alcoholic," *you can say,* "Some things are hard to accept, aren't they?"

When they say, "I understand your child is a real terror at school. Don't you ever discipline him?" *you can say,* "Tell me what you have heard and why you're concerned."

When they say, "Your child is in trouble with the law, and *you're* teaching Sunday school?" *you can say,* "I'm sorry that offends you. Perhaps we should talk about how you feel."

When they say, "I understand your married son is having an affair with another woman. Don't you think you should talk to him and tell him what he is doing is wrong? After all, you *are* his parent," *you can say,* "What our son is doing is very upsetting to us. However, he is a grown man and must live with the consequences of his own decisions."

When they say, "Well, your son may be in jail, but at least you have your other children at home. I hope nothing goes wrong with them," *you can say,* "So do I."

When they say, "I'm sorry to hear your son wandered off from the way you raised him. This must be a shock," *you can say,* "Thank you for caring."[2]

Tend to the Needs of the Rest of Your Family

"I was so emotionally exhausted taking care of my oldest child that there was nothing left for my other children," said one mom I interviewed. "It wasn't until my second-oldest child began showing signs of trouble that I realized something had to change. I decided that I needed to stop attending every court appearance for my oldest son, and begin investing in my other kids as well. I had to take control of my life. I had to forgive myself for where I had failed my oldest son, and work on not repeating those same errors with my other children."

This mother realized the importance of caring for the well-being of *all* her children, which meant that she not pour all her energies into her one wayward child.

While most parents recognize the stress that a rebellious child brings into their lives, they may not realize the extent to which that stress impacts the other family members. All families function as a complete system—a whole made up of interrelated and interdependent parts. The unwritten goal of every family is to bring that system into balance or equilibrium. Like an old-fashioned scale, when something is added to one side, a corresponding adjustment must be made on the other side for it to balance. As a result, individual family members become adept at intuitively sensing what is needed and naturally fulfilling that role.

This can be healthy, as in the case of a single-parent home where the mother becomes breadwinner, the oldest child cooks and keeps watch over the younger children, and the younger children help to clean and perform other essential chores around the house. But when one member suddenly refuses to cooperate, every other member is affected. In time, they all adjust, and often develop new roles as a result, though these new roles can be unhealthy ones. Depending upon the extent and duration of the rebellion, one family member might emerge as the caretaker, another the protector. One becomes an enabler, while another takes on the role of the forgotten child.

When the offending child moves out, is removed, or suddenly becomes better, the system is once again thrown out of balance. We often see this when the rebellious child in a family goes to jail, becomes a Christian, and then exhibits authentic positive change. One would assume that the family would be thrilled, but that is not always the case.

Strangely enough, the problem child was playing an important role in the family system. When the child who had been the focus of everyone's attention and frustration is no longer in that role, other issues with family members are soon unmasked. Problems that had previously been ignored, hidden, or repressed suddenly rise to the surface, including marriage tensions that went undetected as long as all the attention was focused on the problem child.

Here are some things you can do to protect your children from feeling neglected and from taking on an unhealthy role in the family system:

Do fun activities as a family.
Having fun together will help all of you feel relief from some of your daily stresses. Don't let your times with your other children seem like a reward for good behavior, but a celebration of your lives together. This will help ensure they don't conclude that the only way to get your attention is to rebel.

Ask God to be your strength in those times when you have nothing left to give.

Troubled kids consume even more emotional energy than they do time. Though your current situation may be wearing you down, try not to carry your feelings of anxiety over to the rest of the family.

Be aware that your rebellious teen may be influencing younger siblings to engage in negative behaviors.

Your problem child's activities may seem exciting, dangerous, or even glamorous to younger brothers and sisters. Kids often admire older siblings and catch on quickly to the tricks and lies that pervade their older sibling's world. Many of the young offenders we meet in detention centers lament the effects they've had on their brothers and sisters as they see them following their negative example.

To help offset this tendency:

- Be open with your children about the struggles you're having with their brother or sister. They are likely well aware of the situation, so don't ignore it or try to hide it from them. Do this with respect, exhibiting confidence that they will be wise enough to avoid the same pitfalls. Avoid communicating a sense of fear or foreboding over the path they may choose for their futures.

- Ask your children how they feel about the situation that has been created by their sibling, exploring how it has affected them or may affect them in the future. Don't react in anger to their responses, even if they are critical of your behavior. Your children will often have good insights into the problem that you may not have noticed. Showing respect for their opinions will increase the likelihood that they will respect yours.

- Don't communicate any negative feelings you may have toward their sibling. Be honest and realistic, but ask God to clear away any animosity you may be feeling. Such negative feelings can harden a child toward a sibling who may be causing them grief. This only increases family tension and complicates a reconciliation process. Or, if the child admires their sibling, your negative outlook may only spur on their own rebellious leanings.

- Spend as much free time as possible with the younger siblings to keep the lines of communication open and pick up early signs that they may be heading in the wrong direction.

Parenting for the long haul means that you don't ignore your own needs or the needs of other family members while dealing with a rebellious child. Parents who follow this principle will find their homes much healthier and their families more able to survive the stresses caused by wayward children.

Summary

Four proactive principles to protect your marriage and family:

- Invest in your marriage.
- Present a united front to your child.
- Build a support network.
- Tend to the needs of the rest of your family.

Chapter Five

Strategies for Your Own Survival

He will turn the hearts of the fathers to their children,
and the hearts of the children to their fathers.

MALACHI 4:6

Hanne and I had been talking with one of the teens who was living with us, Jermaine, about a particular issue he was struggling with and his need to surrender every area of his life to Christ. He was hearing us, but it just wasn't connecting for him, and we were becoming increasingly frustrated. Finally, we decided to quit talking to him about it and to begin praying fervently about it instead.

Within a week, Jermaine came to us, saying, "I have decided that I really need to give this area of my life over to God. I know that my main focus needs to be God if I'm ever going to really make it."

When will we ever learn? Not only did Hanne and I feel better once we committed to pray for Jermaine, we also got out of the way so God could deal more directly with him.

Prayer is the first of several proactive principles that can protect parents from feeling burned out or completely overwhelmed in their efforts to parent for the long haul.

Invest in the Power of Prayer

I know of no better way to help ourselves—and ultimately our kids—than to entrust them to God. Ephesians 6:12 tells us that our struggle is not against flesh and blood. Spiritual battles must be fought in a spiritual manner. As James 5:16 says, "The prayer of a righteous man is powerful and effective."

While most of us would agree in principle that prayer is the single most powerful force we can release into the lives of our children, sometimes we just don't know how to pray effectively. At other times we struggle with being able to focus our attention on God and his faithfulness. We feel paralyzed and lack the faith and confidence to believe God can do great things.

Since faith comes from hearing God's Word, one of the best ways to bolster our faith is to pray God's Word back to him, personalizing it to our own specific needs and those of our child.

Below are several prayers and promises in Scripture that can encourage parents of a wayward child. Write them on 3x5 note cards so that you can carry them with you, tuck them in your Bible, or post them on your bathroom mirror. Adapt them so they become personal to you when your faith wavers.

I prayed for this child, and the Lord has granted me what I asked of him. So now I give him [her] to the Lord. For his [her] whole life he [she] will be given over to the Lord.

1 SAMUEL 1:27-28

God ... grant them repentance leading them to a knowledge of truth ... that they will come to their senses and escape from the trap of the devil, who has taken them captive to do his will.

2 TIMOTHY 2:25-26

I pray ... that the eyes of your heart may be enlightened in order that you may know the hope to which he has called you, the riches of his glorious inheritance.

EPHESIANS 1:18

"For I know the plans I have for you," declares the Lord, "plans to prosper you and not to harm you, plans to give you hope and a future."

JEREMIAH 29:11

Being confident of this, that he who began a good work in you will carry it on to completion until the day of Christ Jesus.

PHILIPPIANS 1:6

Be strong and courageous. Do not be terrified; do not be discouraged, for the Lord your God will be with you wherever you go.

JOSHUA 1:9

For God did not give us a spirit of timidity, but a spirit of power, of love and of self-discipline.

2 TIMOTHY 1:7

If any of you lacks wisdom, he should ask God, who gives generously to all without finding fault, and it will be given to him.

JAMES 1:5

Be still, and know that I am God.

PSALM 46:10

You might also want to copy the following prayer and pray it daily for you and your child.

Dear God,

I can't parent my child in the way you would have me. It is far beyond my own abilities. But I also know that you have entrusted this child into my care.

I need your help. I need your strength, wisdom, and power. Today I call upon you for the discernment, patience, and love I need to be the parent that you have called me to be.

Please forgive me where I have failed you and my child, and grant me the opportunity to seek forgiveness from those whom I have offended.

Lord, I acknowledge that I cannot control or change my children, and so I release them into your loving care, and pray that your will be done in them.

I also thank you for how this child has revealed a bit more of my own darker side. I ask you to continue to use this painful situation to further mold me into the image of your Son, Jesus.

It's in his name that I ask it. Amen.

Examine Yourself Honestly and Adjust Where Necessary

Parenting a rebellious child has a way of surfacing many of our own unresolved emotional issues. None of us comes empty-handed to the parenting process. We bring a lifetime of experience, and it's not all good. Sometimes we fall into the same destructive patterns our own parents exhibited, patterns that we were determined never to repeat. Other times we do just the opposite of our parents, which can be equally damaging.

If we want to successfully parent for the long haul, we must be willing to confront those things about ourselves that need to be changed. We must be honest about our weaknesses and failures, and then confess them to God and to others whom we may have hurt—particularly our spouse and children. When a parent is willing to ask a child for forgiveness, it not only heals wounds, but models for him or her an appropriate method for righting wrong behavior and choices.

Shortly after Hanne and I had opened our home to troubled teens, I was talking to a friend on the telephone in my office. He asked me how things were going. "It's a lot tougher than I thought it would be," I confessed. "We only have one teen right now, and it's a full-time job just keeping him going. What's it going to be like when we have a houseful?"

No sooner had I gotten the words out of my mouth than I turned around and saw Tony standing in my office doorway. He had heard every word. He grabbed what he was looking for and left, but by the look on his face I knew I had hurt him deeply.

I had to rush off to a speaking engagement, so I wasn't able to talk with him about what had just happened. But while I was driving, I kept thinking about how foolish I had been for having said such hurtful words.

Finally I pulled over along the side of the road to phone Tony. "I'm so sorry for what I said on the telephone, Tony. I didn't mean it that way; I was just having a frustrating day. I couldn't be happier that you're living with us. Will you forgive me?"

He said, "Yes."

When Tony first moved into our home, he had informed us that there were three things he never said: *Please, Thank you,* and *I'm sorry.* But after that experience, saying the words *I'm sorry* came much more easily for him.

Sometimes we don't realize our mistakes as parents until several years later. But even if you realize you were wrong years after the transgression, it's still important to go back and ask for forgiveness.

One father shared this story with me: "Our son Alan has always been a people-person, and is easily influenced by others. By middle school he had begun to exhibit defiant attitudes that were an indication we were in for some difficult years. As he was about to enter high school, he asked to transfer to our local technical high school because his interest was more in the trades than academics. At the time, that particular trade school had a bad reputation for drawing the most rebellious students and was known as a place where drugs were rampant. We said 'no.'

"Well, our hunches about Alan's future were right. He struggled with drugs, failed several classes, and received multiple suspensions.

"It wasn't until several years after he graduated that I

learned he was very bitter toward us for denying him the opportunity to go to technical school, where, in his mind, he could have flourished. He told a mutual friend, 'I was determined to show my parents that I could get into just as much trouble in the regular high school.'

"When I heard that, I immediately called Alan to see if I could take him out for lunch. When we got together I told him what I had heard. 'Can you forgive me, Alan? I did what I did out of fear, and it was wrong. If I could do it again, I would have allowed you to attend the technical school where you could excel in those things you're naturally good at.'

"At that point, Alan had moved in and out of living situations with several girls, was generally living irresponsibly, and had bill collectors hounding him day and night over a loan he had defaulted on. 'Your mother and I have talked a great deal about this. To show you how serious we are, we would like you to give us your loan book. We will begin making payments on that loan,' I told him.

"He gave us the loan book, and neither of us said another word about it, until two years later when he came by and asked for the loan book back. He's been making payments on it consistently ever since. My apology was a watershed moment. Since then, our relationship has been restored to a level we had never enjoyed before. Alan got married and he is a wonderful father to his son. He has also come back to church—something he had refused to do since he was in the tenth grade."

While it's painful to see our own failings and shortcomings exposed at the hands of our children, it can also be the place where God can bring us healing and wholeness.

Another father explained it this way:

I'm starting to understand at least part of the reason why God gave me the teenagers he did. They're tough kids, but God knew I needed tough kids to bring me to the end of myself. Before they became adolescents, I thought I had it made. In regular surgeon-style, I had everything sewn up, so much so that I didn't need God in a practical way. When my kids started to bleed, in a manner of speaking, I went to work to sew them up, too. But nothing I did worked after they reached thirteen. It was the first time my mind and skills weren't enough.

I still have no idea how my kids will turn out, but I've begun to trust the Lord for the strength and wisdom to parent them in a whole new way—a way I never knew was possible. Something had to completely shift inside of me before I could start to love them just the way they are. I think they sense something has changed in me. And I really think that's had more impact on them than anything I could have ever said or done.[1]

No doubt God will use your children to reveal your own flaws as well. Embrace the process as he uncovers those ugly issues. Allow him to do the deep work of refining your life and character.

Nurture Your Own Soul

As part of the preparation work for my doctoral program, I had to undergo a myriad of assessment tests. Some were self-assessment tests and others had to be completed by Hanne. Still others were to be completed by coworkers.

During the first week of residency I was supposed to meet with a psychologist who would interpret the tests for me. I anxiously awaited the results as I watched the counselor check one test against another. When he finally looked up, his first words were, "Scott, do you think you might be depressed?"

Well, when a professional who has just spent a great deal of time examining all your assessment tests asks you that, if you weren't depressed before, you certainly were now! "I ... I don't know. You tell me."

After we had talked for awhile, he suggested, "You may be a bit depressed, but I think it's more likely that the problems you're facing currently in your life and ministry are just a whole lot greater than your current experience with God."

Bingo! He had hit it on the head. The issues I was dealing with daily with the guys in our home loomed so large that they had completely overshadowed my sense of God's presence and power in my life.

I knew I was in trouble, but I also knew why. I wasn't spending adequate time with God, getting my soul nurtured and fed. I began to get away for a half day every week to spend with the Lord. One of the books I read was the fifteenth-century classic, *Imitation of Christ.* In it, Thomas à Kempis remarked how every unrest of heart or distraction of mind stems from one of two realities: either a misdirected affection or an ungrounded fear.[2] I had plenty of both, and could only combat them through rekindling my relationship with Jesus. In spending much more time with him, the reality of his presence eventually became stronger than the realities of the difficulties that surrounded me.

Not surprisingly, parents of troubled adolescents often fall further and further away from a vibrant relationship with Christ. Sometimes it's due to emotional exhaustion, other times to feelings of disillusionment over the lack of change in a child's behavior despite the prayers of his parents and those of a hundred others. If this is true for you, be honest with God. Tell him how you feel. That's authentic and sincere, and he can work with that. But above all, if you hope to have anything of substance at all for yourself, your child, and the other members of your family, you must nurture your own relationship with Christ.

George Whitefield, the powerful preacher of the eighteenth century Great Awakening, once said, "Our churches are dead because those of us who are leading them are dead." When we're dealing with a rebellious child we can easily let it consume our energy, and begin subtly neglecting our own soul. Once this happens, we no longer have the reserves out of which to pray and draw strength from the Lord. We find ourselves fighting a spiritual battle against unseen powers and principalities, but with mere human weapons.

Nurturing one's soul involves more than just spending time with God. It involves taking time to play as well as pray. We need to engage in activities that we enjoy so as not to become consumed with our pain.

One couple described their strategy for survival: "When

Nathan entered the tenth grade we could see that his problems were not going to be solved in the short run. We decided that we needed to begin tending to our own needs as well. We could no longer be held hostage by Nathan's rebelliousness. We would continue to be concerned about Nathan, but not consumed by him.

"One thing we decided to do together was lose weight. Focusing on eating healthier foods not only helped us feel better, it also served to deter some of our energy and gave us a much-needed sense of accomplishment. And exercising became a great anger and stress dissipater."

Identify the kinds of things you need to do to nurture your own soul and to take care of yourself—and then set aside time each day or every week to do those things. Make them a priority for your sake and for the sake of your family.

Engage the Help of a Professional Counselor

If the stresses of dealing with your child have become detrimental to your own emotional well-being and you can no longer cope through your normal support systems, you need to seek professional help.

Counseling doesn't necessarily have to involve a long, drawn-out series of sessions. One or two sessions with a trained and competent counselor may be enough to guide you and let you know you are on a right course.

How can a counselor help me?

Here are some of the benefits that professional counselors can provide:

1. An unbiased perspective. In times of crisis, our ability to see things clearly can be severely impaired. A neutral, credible person can reflect issues in a way that family members or close friends often are unable to.

Mary told me: "I'm a real perfectionist. When I heard the labels the school psychologists had assigned to our son Derrick, I went to work researching it all out.

"'Oh, it says here that this condition is often the result of a child not bonding with his mother. So I'm the reason for his problems,' I reasoned. That put me into a real tailspin. During our weekly session, I explained to our counselor what I had discovered. After hearing me, he said, 'Stop, Mary. There are many factors that have contributed to Derrick being where he is, but your inadequate mothering is not one of them. Yes, we all make mistakes, and none of us is perfect, but you're not the problem.' I needed to hear that. And I needed to hear it from someone of his caliber and expertise."

Experienced counselors can help us see things more objectively. They may be able to help us see the underlying cause of the problem, help us determine how serious it really is, or provide insights into the options we have before us.

2. Identification of contributing factors. In the midst of conflict, it's often difficult to identify the past or current events that are exacerbating or even causing the conflict. A trained counselor can often see issues behind the problem that may be a key in helping us more effectively deal with the situation.

One mother whose son had recently been arrested for vandalism was baffled at the sudden change in her son's behavior. While talking with a counselor, she mentioned that he had met his absentee father by accident in the mall a month earlier. The counselor was able to help the mother and son talk about the significance of that event and how it had affected his subsequent behavior. Although discussing it did not completely heal the pain, it put his actions in a context they both could understand.

3. Help in self-examination. We all possess some unhealthy parenting patterns. Even when we recognize them, some of these patterns are so ingrained in us they seem impossible to change. Other patterns may remain hidden from us unless someone else points them out. While this can be a painful process, it can also lead to help and healing so we are able to minister more authentically to those in our family.

"I went to the counselor looking for a cure for my son," said a father whose son was involved with drugs. "Over the next two months I saw how God was changing me through our counseling sessions. In fact, I even asked to meet with the counselor separately for several sessions. I could see that God needed to deal with my own areas of unresolved pain before I could provide the help necessary for my son."

4. Guidance in making decisions. A wayward child can throw parents into a crisis, inhibiting their ability to think clearly and make wise decisions. One of the counselor's jobs is to help parents gain a sense of balance and perspective so that they make wise decisions for their child and family.

A couple entered the counselor's office right after discovering their daughter in bed with a boy in their home. The father was so enraged that he was unable to sit down, while the mother was just trying to cope with the shock. In a counselor's office they were able to talk through their feelings and gain some perspective on their pain. They realized that this was not the end of the world, nor had they lost their daughter. After they had grieved and dealt with their sense of disappointment, they were able to set a course to regain communication with their daughter and talk through how to handle the issue.

How do I find the right counselor?

How do you figure out who would be a good counselor for you and your child? Here are some questions to consider:

1. Am I comfortable with this person's approach? Ask what kinds of methods she uses and how she determines when to employ them. How much emphasis does she place upon spiritual principles and a reliance on the Holy Spirit? Ask if she includes the whole family in therapy. A counselor who understands family dynamics will have greater insight into your child, while one who focuses solely on the teen may miss issues crucial to the healing process.

2. Is this person recommended by people I trust? Successful counselors should be able to give you names of others who have benefited from their services. But remember that just because a person is a good counselor and helped someone else, doesn't mean he's necessarily right for you. The best recommendation comes from a person who has insight into you as well as into the counselor.

3. Does this counselor have the right training? Some therapists are general practitioners while others have areas of specialization. If possible, find someone who works primarily with families and teens. Where drugs, the occult, learning disabilities, or other specific issues may be involved, try to find a counselor who has some experience in that arena.

4. Does this counselor take a holistic view? Emotional issues are often related to spiritual, physical, and learning problems. Good counselors take into account health issues that may also influence behavior. A counselor who looks at school assessments or doctors' reports may be able to make key connections that will determine the direction for the counseling. At other times a simple, spiritual insight can help provide discernment about seemingly overwhelming problems.

5. Can I afford it? If you don't have insurance, or if a counselor doesn't take your insurance, you may need to look for alternatives. Some pastors are skilled in helping people through problems in the short term. If the issue needs a long-term approach, ask for help in finding an appropriate counselor and various methods for paying for it.

6. How does this person define successful treatment? A good therapist should be working toward some measurable goals so that you can discern progress and know when treatment should end. Three good indications that you may be ready to move on are evidence of the following:

- a growing insight into the issues
- increased ability to cope with the problems
- a new sense of spiritual understanding.

If you just don't seem to be getting anywhere with your counselor, don't be afraid to try another. Make it a matter of earnest prayer. God will direct you.

Choose to Enjoy Your Children

Over the years, Hanne and I have reparented more than thirty troubled teens. Those were some of the toughest days of my life, and, undoubtedly, some of the best. Truly, I would never have known such deep pain or so much joy were it not for the privilege of parenting difficult teens.

Looking back, though, I realize that I often robbed myself of many of the joys simply because I viewed the good times as merely a "lull before the storm." I regret this, and so do other parents I've talked with who did the same.

Never let your love for and enjoyment of your children be overshadowed by the anger, hurt, or frustration they may be causing you. While you need to be attentive and responsive to the issues your child is grappling with, don't allow your current anxieties and mistrust to keep you from creating positive memories together, even though your child will seldom wholeheartedly embrace such activities at the time.

A good friend told me about an outing she had planned to take with her fifteen-year-old daughter. "Tanya and I had been missing each other for several weeks, so when I learned about a series of pancake breakfasts that were taking place on several Saturdays at a rural New England farm, I thought it would be a fun, educational, and inexpensive way to spend a Saturday morning together. The first Saturday we tried to make it happen, Tanya wanted to sleep in. The next Saturday, I had other plans. As the third Saturday approached, it looked as though breakfast on the farm might actually happen.

"When I awoke that morning, I was feeling pressured to get a bunch of errands done, and Tanya was barely awake, never mind dressed, when it was time to leave. I said to her, 'I've changed my mind about going to the pancake breakfast this morning. I've got so many things I have to do. We can try again next Saturday if you want.' She didn't say anything, and I left to tend to my errands.

"A couple of days later, Tanya was having a really bad day. School had been a downer, and she was just in an all-around bad mood. As I was asking her about it she said, 'And how do you think it makes me feel when you tell me you've changed your mind about something we had made plans to do together? It makes me feel like *you* don't care about me either!'

"I had no idea Tanya actually *wanted* to go to that pancake breakfast. I had just assumed I was throwing another idea out there that she was not really interested in at all, but was agreeing merely to please me. I mistakenly thought I was letting her off the hook for doing something 'dorky' with her mom by telling her I had changed my mind. I had no idea how much I had hurt her feelings.

"When we actually did make the trip the next Saturday, Tanya didn't seem too thrilled about the experience, and mostly kept asking when we could go home. But then later that evening, I overheard her talking with a friend on the phone. She was excitedly telling about all the animals and the experience of collecting sap from maple trees and seeing how it was made into syrup. I was really glad that I hadn't allowed my own frustrations about pulling off an event together keep me from putting forth the effort of trying."

Our children are at home for such a short time. While it's tempting to focus more on the difficulties and negative experiences rather than work to create positive ones, don't allow the darkness to prevail. Choose to enjoy those times you do have together and strive to create memories where the light can actually dispel some of the darkness.

Summary

Five proactive principles to help you survive parenthood:
- Invest in the power of prayer.
- Examine yourself honestly and adjust where necessary.
- Nurture your own soul.
- Engage the help of a professional counselor.
- Choose to enjoy your children.

Chapter Six

What Your Child Needs Most

Don't exasperate your children by coming down hard on them. Take them by the hand and lead them in the way of the Master.

EPHESIANS 6:4, THE MESSAGE

When you're in the midst of dealing with the long-term effects of raising a difficult child, you're always looking for a checklist, a *Ten Commandments of Parenting* list you can put on your refrigerator and apply on a daily basis while you wait for the payoff. While there is no such list, there are some proactive principles that indicate when you're on the right track toward providing your child what he or she most needs.

Try to See Things From Your Child's Perspective

Adolescence is a time of great internal and external upheaval. But as irrational as teens can appear, there is usually a reason behind their sometimes maddening behavior. Anxieties, guilt, depression, fear of failure, insecurity, or strained friendships can all contribute to a state of rebellion.

First, adolescents are bombarded with internal stresses. For example, the testosterone levels in a boy's bloodstream rise a hundredfold during puberty.[1] It's not hard to imagine why teenage boys, under the influence of a potent chemical that fuels both sex and aggression, struggle so in making coherent decisions.

Girls' bodies change just as radically. Each year it seems the onset of puberty hits earlier and earlier, making life all the more difficult and confusing for young girls. Girls who mature earlier than their peers have the added pressure of the attention of older boys—attention they are not emotionally or psychologically ready for.

During this period, it is natural for teens to leave many of their parents' values temporarily behind, forming a generational loyalty to one another. This is part of the normal individuation process. When adults challenge the ideas and ideals of youth too quickly, they alienate themselves from their teens all the more.

A good friend of ours, Diane, has raised two daughters as a single mother. The first daughter was a breeze, but Shari was a different story. From her earliest days she seemed to be attracted to the more countercultural side of life. The day she came home with orange spikes in her hair and white makeup on her face, Diane gasped. *Do I say something? Do I ignore it? Do I demand that she reinstate her beautiful blonde hair?!*

Sometimes kids do outlandish things simply to be noticed, and Diane wisely realized she shouldn't ignore such a bold statement from her daughter. So she simply said, "Wow! That's quite a hairdo, Shari. What made you decide to do it?"

"Oh, Mom. It's what my friends are into these days. Do you like it?"

"Like it? Well, it's not exactly what I would have ordered.

But it's not my hair, it's yours."

"Thanks, Mom. I knew you'd understand."

But inside Diane didn't understand at all. What kind of friends was Shari hanging around with, anyway? How much was the divorce impacting some of her bizarre behaviors?

Diane made a wise choice—she asked. She didn't ignore or attack Shari's behavior, she talked openly with her. She asked her the questions that were plaguing her as a mother, all the while assuring her daughter that she was committed to her well-being. Shari responded graciously as well. She admitted that she was struggling with the reasons her father had left and that she didn't feel accepted by mainstream society, especially at church. But she did feel secure in her mother's love.

Diane and Shari went through a lot tougher times than battles over clothes and hairstyles, but now that Shari is in her midtwenties, both mother and daughter consider each other best friends.

In addition to internal pressures, today's teens also face enormous external pressures from a popular culture that is often toxic. A study commissioned by The Carnegie Council on Adolescent Development warns that one in four teens is extremely vulnerable to high-risk behaviors and dangerous lifestyles. The report concludes that today's children are susceptible to "a vortex of new risks ... almost unknown to their parents or grandparents."[2]

In the midst of all of these pressures, our children need to feel that their parents understand their fears, their desires, their feelings, their inexplicable impulses, their frustrations, and their inabilities. When they are convinced of that, real change is possible.

Often, kids can't even verbalize what is stressing them. But if they sense that we are on their side and not against them, then we can at least begin working together. James' advice is timeless. "Be quick to listen, slow to speak and slow to become angry" (Jas 1:19).

Allow Natural Consequences to Take Their Course

The real world operates on natural consequences, yet most parents dispense unrelated punishments when trying to correct a child's behavior. Unfortunately, these punishments aren't productive and can even be detrimental with rebellious teens.

For example, if your son gets a speeding ticket and you ground him for a week, he can see no natural correlation between his behavior and the consequence. Such a consequence only serves to create friction between parent and teen. In the real world, however, people don't get grounded when they get speeding tickets. They have to pay large fines and even larger car insurance premiums, and eventually they lose their licenses.

Far better to say to Speedy Gonzales, "I can agree with you that driving fast is a lot of fun. But as you know, it does have its downfalls. You now have a fine to pay and our insurance rates will likely go up significantly as well. If so, in addition to paying the fine, you'll have to pay the difference in the insurance premium if you want to remain on our insurance policy so you can continue to drive."

When we allow teens to get away with doing wrong by shielding them from the consequences of their behavior, we do them a great disservice. Such action is the very definition of the term *enabling*, which is helping another person to act irresponsibly and get away with it.

Oftentimes however, it's just easier to bail our kids out, so we don't have to see them suffer. For example, if your daughter misses a deadline for signing up for basketball and is told that she can't participate in the sport for the entire season, it might seem easier for you to talk to the athletic director and try to get an exception made than to see your daughter miss an opportunity. But does it really help her in the long run—especially if procrastination has been an ongoing problem for her?

Enforcing consequences is challenging, and parents can be tempted to take the easy way out. Hanne and I have been guilty of this many times. We would ground guys in our home from using the car, only to realize that now we had to transport them to school, to work, to youth group—all activities that we felt they needed to participate in. In reality, we levied a bigger punishment on ourselves than on them. Consequently, those groundings seldom lasted.

Far better to immediately confront the transgression, say you're going to take time to pray about what should be done, and ask the young person to do the same—so that together you can arrive at a consequence that will help them learn the most from the incident. We have often asked the kids living in our home to come up with consequences they felt would teach them the most. Many times the consequences they arrived at were stiffer than what ours would have been. Kids are also much more likely to learn from, and abide by, consequences that are self-imposed.

Do kids always come up with appropriate consequences? No. But then you can say, "I was really hoping we were both committed to seeing how you could best learn and grow through this. But it seems we're not as united on this as I had hoped. Do you want to take another stab at it, or should I come up with a consequence for you myself?" A good consequence is one that, when asked, "Who's making me hurt like this?" forces your child to conclude, "Oh, me."[3]

How far do I let my child fall?

While it is critical to allow the natural consequences of most choices our kids make, some teens are falling in freestyle fashion, and will stop only when they hit bottom. Sometimes that bottom can cause permanent damage to a young person's character, health, or future. Determining how far you should allow your teen to fall before you intervene is a decision that requires great wisdom and sensitivity to the Lord's Spirit.

While I know that each child is different, experience tells me that most teens who have been in and out of trouble may benefit more from spending a night in a detention center than from being bailed out by their parents. Contrary to popular myth, rape and rampant drug use are not necessarily part of the lockdown initiation. A night of incarceration can serve as a much-needed wake-up call for many teens.

The bottom line is this: To rescue adolescents from natural consequences does not always do them a service. Rather, it may retard their emotional development, and in the end, keep them in perpetual childhood.

Setting behavior standards for and with your child up front lessens the likelihood of conflict between you when a standard is not met. With agreed-upon standards in place, if your teen strays you can more easily say, "I'm surprised you would make that choice, but I must honor our agreement."

Love and Accept Without Condoning Sin

Historically, Christians have followed St. Augustine's age-old charge to love the sinner while hating the sin. In our post-modern times, however, to be tolerant demands that we embrace both the individual and their lifestyle, regardless of how sinful it may be.

It isn't easy to accept a person whose behavior is intolerable. For example, a Christian parent might well reason about their son who has been charged with vandalism: "I can't accept or respect him. It would be like condoning his behavior, and I hate the choices he's made." But loving and accepting our children is not the same as agreeing with their behavior. Of course, our natural desire is to want their conduct to change. But is that God's greatest agenda for them?

A well-known radio preacher tells the story of receiving a disturbing phone call at the office from his wife one morning. She had just discovered that their teenage son had come home drunk the night before. It was the first time anything like this had happened, and they were both very upset.

The father got in his car and raced home. "How could he do this to me?" he thought. "He's been such a leader at church and in youth group. He's warned his friends about avoiding such traps and now he's fallen into the same thing. How hypocritical!"

Then he began thinking about the embarrassment this would bring upon him as a pastor, speaker, author, and radio preacher. What would people say about him when he couldn't even manage the affairs of his own family? The more he pondered, the angrier he became. It was a good thing he had a long drive home.

After venting his frustrations, he was finally able to pray for his son and his own response. As he did, the question he kept hearing God ask him was, "What is your desire for your son? Is it simply that he never drink again? If so, then deal harshly with his behavior, and hopefully he won't dare do it again.

"Or is it your greatest desire that he learn to grow in the grace and knowledge of the Lord Jesus Christ? If that's your goal, then you need to handle the situation quite differently."

By the time the father got home, his son was waiting for him. Nervous and shaking, he didn't dare meet his father's eyes.

"Son," his father began, "Son, I really love you. I hate what you did, but I want you to know how much I love you."

Before he could go any further, his son broke down and began crying profusely. "Oh, Dad. I've *heard* you say that a hundred times. But today is the first day I *know* that it's true. I'm sorry. I'm so sorry. I don't ever want to do that again."[4]

This father understands the meaning of parenting for the long haul. God's will prevailed that day because a father put his son's needs ahead of his own feelings of embarrassment.

Loving and accepting a child doesn't negate the need to confront sinful behavior; on the contrary. But for the confrontation to be effective, we need to have an intact relationship. We must work hard to insure that our children understand that our confrontation is directed at their wrong behavior and not them.

Never make "good behavior" a prerequisite for your affection. It's a condition that even God doesn't demand. To unconditionally love *despite* sinful behavior makes room for God's miraculous intervention.

I like what one Christian mother shared about her response

to her nineteen-year-old son's choice to live with his girlfriend:

"When Alex came home to tell us he'd moved in with Claudia, I burst into tears, even though I'd half expected it for months. I told him we could never approve, but of course, he knew that. I also told him that because he was our son, we would keep loving him no matter what happened. But accepting his girlfriend was impossible as far as I was concerned. I didn't even want to talk to her.

"When I expressed my feelings to my daughter, she said, 'Mom, it's very possible Alex and Claudia will get married someday. If that happens, I want to like and get along with my sister-in-law.'

"Christmas promised to be an awkward time," she continued. "But when I learned Alex wanted to bring Claudia over to our house for our family celebration, I decided to make her feel welcome. We spent as much money on gifts for her as we did for our own daughter.

"We had a beautiful Christmas day together as a family. We were all able to relax and enjoy what I had feared might be a strained experience. I know my feelings were accurate because as Alex and Claudia said their good-byes at the door, Claudia gave my husband a big hug. Then she came to me and gave me a hug as well.

"As I put my arms around her to squeeze back, my emotions welled up inside me. I didn't want to let go. After they left, I tried to analyze my feelings. It was as though my deliberate acts of acceptance—the sharing of a Christmas meal, the giving of gifts—had released in me a surge of loving acceptance. For the first time I was really able to care about Claudia.

"Not long after that Claudia said to me, 'Your family is so

close. I wish my family could be like that.' At that point, I knew our attitude of acceptance was making a big difference, not only on her, but on our son as well."[5]

Unconditional love, when put into action by faith and God's power, almost always yields supernatural results.

Look for Opportunities to Affirm Your Child

"Last week we received short notice from a realtor that she was bringing over a prospective buyer for our house," said one mother I interviewed. "My daughter Christie was at work, so I had to tidy up her room. I emptied the trash, picked up her clothes, and put a newly-washed quilt on the bed. It had a small tear in the center of it, so to cover it up, I casually tossed a paperback book on top of it. The book was one her sister had recently read for a school book report about a misfit boy.

"When Christie came home from work, she went upstairs to her bedroom as usual, without speaking to me. She had been feeling very insecure and touchy lately, and angry about our need to move and leave our home. A minute later, she stormed down the stairs and in a loud voice demanded to know: "*Who* put that book—*A Child Called It*—on my bed? What's *that* supposed to mean?!"

Christie's reaction revealed just how insecure she was feeling about herself and the situations in her life. It also helped this mother realize that she needed to focus far more on Christie's good qualities, even in the midst of difficulties.

Some parents actually feel it would be wrong to joke around or have fun with their child when there are big issues hanging over their heads. But your child already knows how you feel once you've said it. So why not leave it at that and not seek to punish through silence or harshness? Overwhelming guilt and shame have always been lousy motivators.

Gaze at strengths and glance at weaknesses.

I learned early on with the kids in our home that if I condemned them with my words or actions, they grew insecure, and I wasn't able to effectively work through any difficult issues with them. But if I genuinely affirmed them in the areas where they were doing well, I could address almost any area of concern and greatly minimize the conflict.

When they're already feeling badly about themselves, children can interpret our every gesture as targeting them directly. The problem escalates all the more for the child who is seen as a chronic troublemaker. Many kids develop a failure complex that can run pretty deep by the time they reach their teenage years, and they begin to feel more comfortable with failure than with success. After all, failure is at least familiar.

A good friend of mine who leads a large ministry today told me, "Growing up I was always the 'bad boy.' That was how I got attention. But now, as an adult, it is still a role in which I feel strangely at home. In a twisted sort of way, I'm more comfortable in that role than I am in the role of a leader and positive person. To tell you the truth, success scares me. It's something I have to work on all the time."

We need to help our children see that they are not "bad kids." Rather, they're good kids who occasionally do bad things.

Empower your children by believing in their ability to make good choices.

In my senior year of college I had to make a choice between two job offers. One was several states away. The other was in my hometown. I had refrained from asking my parents for advice, mostly because I already knew what they would say: "Just take the job here. Then you can move back home with us for awhile until you can get on your feet and afford your own place." I didn't want to hear that.

Yet there I was, the day before I had to make a decision, and I had no idea what to do. Finally at 10:30 that night, I broke down and called my parents to get their opinion.

I was shocked when they said, "We really don't know what you should do, Scott. But we do know that you hear from the Lord, and we're confident that you will make the right choice." They caught me completely off guard. Now the pressure was on me. I had to hear from the Lord. And their believing in me empowered me to do just that.

I ended up accepting the job back in my hometown. I even moved back home for a while. It was, without a doubt, the right decision. But I also know that had my parents tried to convince me to move back home, I would have chosen the other job.

My parents empowered me with their confidence in my decision-making ability. By not pushing their views on me, they served to keep the lines of communication open.

Let me share with you a process we used to help the guys in our home learn how to make better decisions. These young men often said they felt trapped, as if they had no options about major decisions they were facing. But in reality, they did have options. So Hanne and I would talk with them about what their options were. Some were good options and some not so good. But by engaging them in this kind of discussion, we helped them think through and articulate the pros and cons of each choice.

We would then point out some of the good choices they had made in the past. We would say something like this: "We know you have the ability to hear from God, and we believe you will hear from him again in this situation. We're not going to make this decision for you. We're entrusting you with it, and we really believe you'll do the right thing."

Most of all we tried not to lecture; we let the teens do most of the talking. We encouraged them to express their ideas and insights and use us as a sounding board.

Did this process guarantee that every teen made wise decisions? Of course not. But if one made a poor decision, we could say, "We were surprised about the choice you made. It didn't seem consistent with where you were going and what we know you to be capable of doing. What do you think happened?" Sometimes the process of talking through a bad choice contributes more to our children's learning and maturity than making good choices in the first place.

Help your children understand and operate out of their own unique gifts and abilities.

In one survey in which high school students were asked what they felt was the biggest problem with their generation, their number one response was *not having anything important to do.*[6]

As Christians we can assure our children that God has a specific plan and purpose for their lives. Jeremiah 29:11 says, he has "plans to prosper [them] and not to harm [them], plans to give [them] hope and a future."

Yet many kids who grow up in Christian homes assume God's only purpose for them is to look and act like all the other people in church, whom they perceive to be dull and boring. When teens get involved in service projects and mission trips, this misperception is often challenged. We've taken the kids in our home on trips to Mexico, Haiti, Ukraine, Ireland, the Dominican Republic, and all over the United States. Such experiences not only expose them to those who are far less fortunate, they also allow them to be a force for good in the life of someone else. For many troubled teens, this can be a turning point.

When we asked Michael, who had lived with us for nearly a year, what kind of mission trip he was interested in, none of the traditional ones seemed to capture his interest. "I don't know," he sighed, "I guess I've always kind of wanted to work with disabled people. Is there anything I can do like that?" We contacted a friend who ran a one-week summer camp for disabled adults. She needed full-time personal care attendants for each attendee and met with Michael.

That turned out to be the best week of Michael's life. He could hardly wait to call home to tell us about his adventures with John, the autistic man he was assigned to. When Michael returned home, he said, "You know, this is the first time I've felt like there was a purpose for my life. I think I've finally found the reason I was born."

Scripture clearly teaches that the Holy Spirit has given each of us spiritual gifts, which are listed in Romans 12:6-8, 1 Corinthians 12:8-10, 28, and Ephesians 4:11. But most teenagers are too insecure and self-conscious to recognize their gifts, concluding instead that they were probably "passed over" when such gifts were being doled out. It is our responsibility as parents to help our kids discover their gifts, to educate them in how to use them, and to provide them with opportunities to exercise them.

Don and Katie Fortune have developed a spiritual gifts questionnaire designed specifically for youth in their book, *Discover Your Children's Gifts*.[7] The book also lists 180 different careers and job possibilities and which are best suited for each gift. It is a good resource for parents of teens.

Proverbs 20:18 says, "Where there is no vision [no redemptive revelation of God], the people perish" (AMPLIFIED). As young people begin to understand who God has uniquely created them to be, they also begin to gain a vision for their lives. They have something bigger to say "yes" to than all the things we're trying to get them to say "no" to. Frankly, until this happens, our interactions with them are mostly on the level of "sin management."

Expose Your Children to Other Adults Who Believe in Them

Other adults can contribute greatly to the character and decision-making process of our children, particularly once they reach the age of thirteen. This is the time when involvement in a good youth group is essential, as teens are beginning to detach from parents and form their own independent attachments.

The reality of teenage individuation can frighten or threaten some parents. I've even seen some try to sever a son or daughter's healthy relationship with another adult. Unfortunately, such behavior can harm a child's development and often results in further alienation between parent and child. If this rings true for you, ask God to change your heart. I know from experience just how positive an impact other adults can have on your child's character and development.

One of the best experiences I had during my junior high school years was to live with and work for a friend of my parents during the summers. Larry operated several farms in southern Minnesota and was a man I idolized.

One evening when my parents were over visiting, I went to bed before they left. Assuming that I was asleep, my mother asked Larry a question. "How do you think Scott's going to turn out?"

I had heard her question, and was straining to hear Larry's reply. I'll never forget the words he said: "Someday Scott will be the president of General Motors." I don't think I slept all night. I felt so good. It was the first compliment that I can remember receiving from anyone outside my family. And the fact that he had said it, not knowing that I was listening, made it even more powerful. Though I always knew that my parents believed in me, I needed to know at least one other person believed in me as well.

The apostle Paul knew the power of this kind of relationship and actively pursued such a role with several people. He even referred to Timothy, Titus, and Onesimus as "sons." To some of the Christians in Corinth he said, "You do not have many fathers, for in Christ Jesus I became your father through the gospel" (1 Cor 4:15). To those in Thessalonica he said, "We dealt with each of you as a *father* deals with his own children, encouraging, comforting and urging you to live lives worthy of God, who calls you into his kingdom and glory" (1 Thes 2:11-12, emphasis added).

Paul was not attempting to replace *anybody's* earthly father. He was speaking of a *deeper* level of commitment and discipleship. I believe that for young people to develop into healthy adults, they need to know that at least one adult outside of their parents really cares for them and believes in them.

Seek Professional Help If Needed

Just as you may benefit from the help of a trained counselor, so might your troubled teen. I encourage you to seek professional help for your child:

- when he or she has been on a downward slide for at least three months, with no improvement in sight
- when there has been a dramatic change in his or her mood or behavior, indicating that something out of the ordinary is happening.[8]

If either of these are true for your child, don't wait to get help! (See chapter nine for more information about specific problems that often require professional help.)

Know That Your Children Want Your Help

Many parents wonder if their kids really *want* their help. Believe me—they do. One major study revealed that while kids do go to each other first for advice, they don't trust it. Overwhelmingly, the youth surveyed indicated they would prefer to go to their parents or other adults first, but they did not believe they had a relationship with them that allowed them to talk openly about their problems.[9]

Another survey asked teens to rank those having "a lot of influence on their thinking and behavior." Here is what they said:

parents	78%
friends	51%
the Christian faith	48%
the Bible	44%
brothers/sisters	40%
teachers	34%
church pastors/priests	27%
music	25%
television	13%
movies	10%
politicians	6%[10]

Parents tend to think it's only "other" kids who respect and listen to their parents. But I'm always amazed that when I do a Bible study on *heroes* in juvenile jails and ask kids to name their biggest hero, almost without exception they say "my mother." Just as those mothers would have been surprised to hear their children describe them that way, we can all assume that we play a much bigger role in our children's lives than they let us know on a daily basis.

I met Traci at a youth retreat. Like many teens today, she was obviously overly stressed in a number of areas of her life. At the end of our conversation I asked if she had shared any of her concerns with her parents. "No, they already have enough problems of their own. They don't have time for my problems, too."

I happen to know Traci's parents, and recognized this as a classic case of misperception. Just as she assumed her parents were too preoccupied to listen to her, they felt Traci wasn't interested in engaging them in conversation.

Parents: assume that your children really do want to be with you, prayerfully watch for those key moments when they are ready to talk, and then drop everything to be available to them. This time is well-spent, as parents who foster honest and open dialogue with their children tend to experience less long-term rebellion.

As you begin to implement these proactive principles, you will find that you are more effective in dealing with the daily crises that emerge with your challenging child. While the implementation of such principles cannot guarantee immediate change, they do help set in motion a more healthy way of addressing the needs of your children. And in the long run, that always pays back dividends.

Summary

Seven proactive principles for parenting rebellious teens:
- Try to see things from your child's perspective.
- Allow natural consequences to take their course.
- Love and accept without condoning sin.
- Look for opportunities to affirm your child.
- Expose your children to other adults who believe in them.
- Seek professional help if needed.
- Know that your children want your help.

Chapter Seven

Keeping a Spark of Faith Alive

God ... grant them repentance leading them to a knowledge of the truth ... that they will come to their senses and escape from the trap of the devil, who has taken them captive to do his will.

2 TIMOTHY 2:25-26

"One Sunday morning at church I couldn't find my son anywhere," recalled one pastor. "I looked all over, and then saw him sitting alone in the car in the parking lot. As I marched out there I felt like yelling, but instead asked, 'Marc, what are you doing out here?'

"'These people don't like me, Dad. They expect me to be something I'm not just because I'm your son.' I knew he was right. Punk rock hair with umpteen earrings made him quite suspect. And I had experienced my own share of angry and disappointed looks as well whenever he entered the church. But Carol and I had made a decision years earlier to not major on the minors with our children. Hairstyle and fashion were not major issues for us, though they clearly were for many in our church.

"As I sat with my son in the car that morning, I knew I had a choice to make. Would I side with him or with those who were opposed to how he looked?

"I renewed my vow to put him above the way his behavior affected people's opinions of me. It's a decision I'm so thankful I made. Though my son is still not attending church, our relationship is still intact."

It's wonderful to be able to preserve our relationship with our child, but how do we ensure that his or her experience of faith becomes vibrant rather than soul-killing—as is so often the case with challenging children who grow up in the church?

While we can't control whether or not our kids ultimately embrace the Lord, we can pray and strive to create an environment where God's Spirit can capture their hearts. For when he does, our children no longer believe simply because they were taught to believe, but because they have personally encountered the Living God and have chosen him for themselves. Working to create such an environment is what this chapter is all about. Consider the suggestions that follow.

Live Out Authentic Faith Before Your Child

Judges 13 tells of a man, Manoah, and his wife who were unable to have children. One day an angel appeared to Manoah's wife and said, "You are sterile and childless, but you are going to conceive and have a son" (v. 3). Then the angel proceeded to instruct this soon-to-be mother on how she should begin to alter her lifestyle.

Overwhelmed by the prospect of being entrusted with a boy who was destined to "begin the deliverance of Israel from the hands of the Philistines," Manoah cried out to God. "O Lord, I beg you, let the man of God you sent to us come again to teach us how to bring up the boy who is to be born" (vv. 5, 8).

Amazingly, his request was granted! When the angel reappeared, the couple had all sorts of questions about the rules they ought to enforce with their new wonder child. Once again, the only instructions the angel gave were about how they, as parents, should live their lives.

This story underlines an important truth: the most significant thing we can do to shape our child's faith is to model an authentic relationship with God. Kids have always picked up far more by watching what their parents do than by listening to their parents' instructions.

Because our children learn so much through observing us, it is important that we allow them to see us openly dealing with our struggles as well as our joys. Why? Because they, too, will face their own deep struggles. When they do, they'll look back, trying to recall examples of how *we* dealt with our hardships. If they saw their parents trusting God and can remember how God was faithful, they will likely trust him, too.

My wife naturally applies her faith to difficult circumstances, and believes she does so largely because of the way her parents handled their struggles when she was a little girl. As missionaries to Denmark, her parents would occasionally take their family to the United States on furlough. For one such trip when Hanne was nine, they paid the initial deposit required to book the tickets and were supposed to pay the remainder at a later date. But some emergency needs came up, and suddenly they didn't have the money to pay the remainder on the tickets. Hanne remembers that her father explained the situation to all of them so that they could pray diligently about it as a family.

The day arrived when the remainder was due, and they still didn't have the necessary funds. The family gathered once again that morning to pray that God would provide. Before they had finished praying, the mailman arrived. Excitedly, her father went to retrieve it. But there were no checks there. What would they do now?

Her parents again gathered the family to pray. Later that day the mailman came back—something that just doesn't happen, even in Denmark! He had one lone envelope. In it was a cashier's check for just the amount of money they needed. The family still, to this day, has no idea where the money came from. The only one they had told of their need was God. What an impression the experience left on a nine-year-old little girl!

It takes only one parent's faith to positively influence a child. Acts 16:1 explains that Timothy's mother was both a Jew and a Christian and his father was a nonbelieving Greek. But when Paul wrote to Timothy in 2 Timothy 1:5, he traced Timothy's "sincere faith" back to Timothy's mother, Eunice, and his grandmother, Lois. In spite of all the other negative influences Timothy may have been exposed to, the godly influence of a mother and grandmother prevailed.

So hang in there. Faith is not on equal grounds with sin. God is stronger than evil, and he can use your sincere faith more powerfully in the life of your child than you may imagine.

Give Your Child Opportunities to Genuinely Encounter Christ

I remember listening to the young people at our church describe their summer mission trip. "God was really there! I've been going to church all my life but this was the first time I knew God was really real!" Kids today need more than just to know about God, they need to encounter and experience him in a way that connects personally with them.

When I was in high school, we were told that if our friends were going to consider the claims of Christ, we had to present a logical argument for our faith. Thus, we spent lots of time studying apologetics. For teens living in these postmodern times, however, understanding isn't believing. Seeing or feeling is believing.

Camps and retreats offer tremendous potential for kids to encounter Christ. Here they are removed from their normal environment and exposed to God's presence in an intensified setting. I have often seen God completely alter the course of a young person's life in less than forty-eight hours on a weekend retreat. This does not mean an instantaneous makeover, of course, but for many it can be the beginning of a whole new direction for their lives.

Creating unique opportunities for our teens to encounter Christ is very important. But what about church? Should you require your teen to attend church?

This is a difficult question and a big concern for Christian parents. Some try to force their children to attend church and in the process drive them further away from God. Others don't give enough guidance or emphasize the importance of church involvement, prematurely giving children the option to not attend.

But most parents I interviewed were in between these two extremes. Some allowed their teens to attend a different church or youth group than the one they themselves attended.

One family said they gave each of their high school-aged children the choice of attending any two of three options: church, Sunday school, or youth group. Though their oldest two were very rebellious in their later teenage years, they never rebelled against church because they felt they had a choice in the matter.

But what about when your teen refuses to attend church altogether? This can be heartbreaking. Still, as one Christian leader told me, "There's life beyond church when it comes to your child's spiritual journey. I think it was important for my son to see the tremendous value we placed upon the community of faith, but when the fight over going to church became a bigger issue than that, we let it go. At different times he would express a desire to go to church, especially at those real low times, and we made every effort to bring him where he would feel most comfortable. I wish I could say that he attends church now as a young adult. Currently he does not. But we have a good relationship, and he still professes a love for God. And I believe church will come, too, in time."

Another friend in ministry was telling me of some of the struggles he was having with his oldest daughter, Kelly. She had completely abandoned her faith and refused to go to church. Instead, her life was being consumed with alcohol, drugs, and a destructive boyfriend and peer group.

Kelly's parents prayed for her for months. That summer the family all went together on a family vacation. As part of their trip, they attended a church that had been experiencing an unusual outpouring of God's power. They had been holding nightly meetings for several weeks. God's Spirit radically got hold of Kelly as she spent several hours weeping at the altar. The family adjusted their vacation schedule and attended church services for several more nights, at their daughter's request. It's now been over a year and Kelly's life is still moving forward with remarkable zeal for the Lord. She discovered the mighty truth of Psalm 84:10: "Better is one day in your courts than a thousand elsewhere."

If you have exposed your children to authentic faith, they will not forget what they have heard and experienced. Recently, I spent some time with one of the first boys who used to live with us. He had fallen a long way from God and was just starting to make his way back. During our conversation he told me, "Even while I was doing bad, I couldn't forget what I had experienced through those mission trips and youth retreats. It used to haunt me day and night to know what I was missing now. I finally couldn't keep buying the lie that sin was fun and following God was boring. It was those memories that eventually drove me back to God again."

No matter what happens after an authentic encounter with Christ, a kid can never completely deny that God is real. They will be able to say as Job did, "My ears had heard of you but now my eyes have seen you" (Jb 42:5).

Give Your Child Back to God

Psychologists often talk about the necessity of conflict for teenagers to develop into healthy adults. In fact, without such struggles, parents would have difficulty helping their children leave the nest and move toward independence.

The feeling a parent has for a child is part of the definition of the Hebrew word *racham* that is translated "compassion." It means "to soothe, cherish, love deeply like parents; the kind of feeling small babies evoke." Hanne described this kind of feeling when she would hold our children as babies, saying, "It felt like I was going to explode on the inside!"

God retains that intense feeling toward us all. Why? Because he never has to let us go. He's not rearing us to be independent of him. He's not rearing us to leave home. He is rearing us to come home![1]

But as parents we must let our kids go. They are given to us as a temporary trust from God. They are "ours" only in the sense that God counts on us to love them, discipline them, and train them. They were not given to us so that we could boast of their good points, any more than we should be ashamed of their failures. We are temporarily watching over the development of other human beings who belong to God, and whose destiny will ultimately be decided between each of them and God alone.

The older our children get, the more we are called to relinquish them. But to relinquish is not to abandon. Rather, it is giving them back to God, and in so doing, taking our hands off them. It does not mean that we stop caring and praying. It does not mean neglecting our responsibilities toward them or relinquishing the authority needed to fulfill those responsibilities. Relinquishment means releasing our need to control, which arises out of our fears or selfish ambitions.[2]

When they turn eighteen years of age, our children are technically adults. They are no longer our responsibility—as much as it may seem or feel like it. The future holds many things, especially for children determined to continue in their rebellion. There are some things they just need to learn for themselves—in the same way we needed to. To continue to allow their rebellion to control our lives is not healthy for them or for us. Of course, we always leave a door open, but we release them nonetheless. God is faithful. And we can be assured that he will be faithful in the lives of our children as well.

God has entrusted us as parents with the most important relationship our children will have in their growing-up years. How we fulfill that role will greatly influence the kind of spouse or parent they will someday be. Even more importantly, the way we relate to them now influences how they will come to view God himself.

Summary

Three ways to help keep the spark of faith alive in your child:

- Live out authentic faith before your child.
- Give your child opportunities to genuinely encounter Christ.
- Give your child back to God.

Chapter Eight

The Death of a Dream

*We were under great pressure, far beyond our ability to
endure ... but this happened that we might not rely on
ourselves but on God.*

2 CORINTHIANS 1:8-9

Rebellious children often present their parents with crisis situations. Sometimes the crisis comes unexpectedly and with full intensity: the son or daughter runs away, declares a change in sexual orientation, gets arrested, or announces an unplanned pregnancy. Other times it comes gradually as he or she becomes increasingly enmeshed in a negative peer culture, continually struggles with drugs or alcohol, exhibits a persistent lack of effort at school, or expresses no desire for spiritual things.

Either way, the crisis represents a loss. It may be the loss of the dreams you once had for your child—a slow death of your hopes for his or her future. Or it may spark the realization that this one child has threatened your own sense of stability, self-image, and sense of well-being. Will you ever know peace and tranquillity again?

Listen to how one father describes the pain that memories of a more innocent time can conjure:

When she tended that wounded bird, you wondered, "Will she be a veterinarian?" When he hit that home run, you thought, "Maybe he'll be an athlete!" Playing dress-up and house made you envision a wedding day and grandchildren. Good report cards conjured up images of doctors' scrubs or suits and ties. Perhaps most poignant were the moments when your child's voice rang out pure and high in the singing of a hymn or the praying of a prayer, and you saw his or her future as a committed child of God.[1]

When our dreams for our child are tarnished or shattered, parenting for the long haul means embracing the grief process, reaching out to others, and taking steps toward reconciliation so we can enjoy the future and have hope for a continued relationship with our child.

Embracing the Grief Process

The Shock Stage

Our first reaction to any loss is shock. Feelings of numbness, disorientation, and being overwhelmed are all normal. Some of us try to recover quickly what was lost while others may feel completely immobilized.

When the loss is due to death or some other tragedy, this stage might last from several hours to a few days or more. But when you are grieving the loss of hopes and dreams for your child, this stage can last considerably longer as more and more things previously hidden are exposed, or your child's actions continue accelerating down a steadily destructive path.

Making logical, coherent decisions while in the shock stage is difficult. Anger, hurt, and self-protection take precedence over a rational long-term perspective. Yet parents are frequently forced to quickly make major decisions about a rebellious child: *Should I require her to leave our home? Do we commit him to a residential drug treatment program? Do we bail him out or let him stay in jail?* When we need to make such decisions quickly, it's critical that we have trusted and supportive friends or professionals with whom to process our thoughts and feelings.

The Denial Stage

The second stage of grief is denial. During this stage, your feelings will likely be the strongest and ugliest and may ricochet from one extreme to another. One minute you feel intensely angry and betrayed; the next finds you sad, ashamed, and feeling personally responsible for all that has happened. Overlying all is an overwhelming sense of desperation, confusion, and helplessness. If that were not enough, most parents of wayward teens add guilt to the mix for even having such feelings.

Some personalities detach in the midst of such pain, saying, "He's made his bed, now he's going to have to lie in it." Others want to rescue: "Maybe if I step in and get him out of this jam, he'll finally have learned his lesson, and we can get back to how things used to be." Such thinking is normal. Don't be too hard on yourself.

In this stage, it is even more critical than in the first stage to have supportive friends and relatives—people who can listen to your pain without needing to respond and give advice. You may also need them to give tangible assistance such as arranging rides for the other children, making meals, setting up appointments, etc. These are all overwhelming tasks for a parent who is consumed and exhausted.

The length of time spent in the denial stage varies among different personalities and in relationship to the extent of the crisis. While people typically spend days in the first stage, the denial phase will more likely take weeks.

The Acceptance Stage

In the acceptance stage, parents are beginning to possess a more positive attitude about the future, even though they may still experience periods of depression. You're able to better focus on the needs of your other children, your spouse, your job, and perhaps even have more hopeful prospects for your wayward son or daughter.

In this stage, one begins to detach from what was lost. Notice, this is not a detachment from the child, but from the dream you once held about what this child would be. More reliable and healthy attachments can now form, such as a deeper relationship with the Lord, one's spouse, a support group, or even a ministry to reach out to others.

While it is not wise to make major decisions alone in the first two grief stages, parents in the acceptance stage are much more capable of engaging in wise decision-making and problem-solving. In this phase you are most open to—and in dire need of—guidance from the Scriptures as well as personal spiritual insights.

Even so, there may be "trigger" experiences that cause sad feelings to resurface. As one father explains, "Going to church and seeing whole families sitting together is still difficult for me. Church is the toughest hour of my week, as my son is now twenty-four years old but still is a long way from the Lord. We haven't sat together in church as a family since he was sixteen."

The Readjustment Stage

It is in this fourth and final readjustment stage that new hope begins to appear. Self-confidence returns, and for many, a new dimension of God-confidence emerges as well. In fact, anyone who possesses a deep, substantive faith has likely been down this path a time or two. Hear it in the words of Job as he speaks to God near the end of his great trial:

> I know that you can do all things; no plan of yours can be thwarted. You asked, "Who is this that obscures my counsel without knowledge?" Surely I spoke of things I did not understand, things too wonderful for me to know.... My ears had heard of you but now my eyes have seen you.
>
> JOB 42:2-3, 5

Crises present opportunities to gain new strengths and new perspectives on life and the chance to chart new directions. As your thinking becomes clearer, you are also able to make wiser decisions—even wiser than had you never gone through such a grief process at all.

While everyone who experiences a crisis goes through the same four stages, the timing and intensity of these stages differs for each person. A husband, wife, and each child in the family may be at completely different stages from one another. The ways in which they act out their feelings will vary as well.

One may withdraw, while another talks excessively. Some become emotionally fragile, while others suffer more physically. It's important to be sensitive to one another, allowing each to grieve individually for what they have lost, and yet be there to support them in the process.[2]

Reaching Out to Others

If your child has catapulted your family into a crisis situation, your first instinct may be to hide from everyone. You may feel embarrassed, paralyzed by the shock of what's being uncovered, or just plain exhausted from telling the same story over and over again. Despite how you feel, don't isolate yourself during this time.

Once word gets out about your crisis, you'll receive a lot of phone calls, letters, and e-mail from concerned friends and acquaintances. How do you respond?

You might consider writing a letter like the sample one on the following page, then making photocopies to give to friends, relatives, acquaintances, or anyone who asks.

Dear Friend,

By now you have probably heard that we're experiencing some difficulty with _____. As you can imagine, this has been very difficult for our entire family. As parents, our emotions vacillate between guilt and anger, often within the same hour. We also struggle with feelings of humiliation and embarrassment as news of our son's [daughter's] behavior becomes more public.

We're sending this letter to ask you to pray with us. While we don't have the energy to explain our situation over and over, we desperately need your friendship and prayers—not just us, but _____ as well. We take great comfort in having a God who can intervene and do what we can't humanly pull off.

Feel free to keep asking us how we're doing. You may feel uncomfortable bringing it up, just as we often do, but in times like these we need one another more than ever. So please don't withdraw from us just because you may not know what to say. Sometimes we may need a listening ear to process all we're going through; at other times we'll want to talk about anything but that.

You, like us, may be tempted to wonder what went wrong. We wish we knew, but thus far God hasn't revealed that to us. We are trusting that he will eventually bring good out of this. In the meantime, we're trying to respond in love, and make wise decisions for the long-term health of _____ and the rest of our family.

Thanks for being there for us. We're so thankful that we don't have to walk through this alone.

Sincerely,

The proactive step of writing this kind of a letter can be a positive step toward reaching out to others, engendering much-needed prayer support and helping you feel less shameful and victimized. Be sure to avoid mentioning details that would embarrass your child. You will need to process your own thoughts and feelings, but this letter is not the appropriate vehicle for that. Consider having a close and trusted friend or pastor review the letter with you before you send it.

Who should receive such a letter? The recipients should be those friends and family members you would normally call if you had the time and energy. A church newsletter or Christmas card list is far too broad an audience.

Taking Steps Toward Reconciliation

Once you have processed your feelings and forgiven your child, you are poised to be able to walk through the stages of reconciliation. I say *poised* because complete reconciliation demands the willing participation of both parent and child. Nonetheless, we can, by an act of faith and obedience to God's principles, lay the groundwork for these stages to be ultimately realized.

Clarify the conditions of the relationship.

To move into the first stage of reconciliation assumes that parents have at least begun to deal with the anger they feel toward their son or daughter. Underlying issues of self-protection or a need to further punish the child stand in the way of taking the risk to forge ahead to rebuild the relationship.

Complete reconciliation also assumes there has been a change in the parent-child relationship. Sometimes this change involves the child moving out of the home, either voluntarily or at the request of a parent. If this is the case, there may be feelings of anger, betrayal, or abandonment that must be addressed before the relationship can be rebuilt. On the other hand, feelings of relief may also prevail, as the tensions precipitated by living together in conflict have disappeared.

Communicate that your love and concern for your child is not marred by the pain you have experienced as a family. At the same time, clarify what conditions the child must agree to before living in your home once again.

One pastor who had to make the difficult decision to ask his eighteen-year-old son to leave their home told me: "We made sure Tim always knew how much we loved him and wanted him in our home. But we had also made the standards and rules for living in our house very clear. We were asking him to leave because of his disobedience and continued criminal activity. Ultimately Tim's leaving our home was a direct result of decisions he was making, but we left the door open for him to come back.

"Six months later, Tim called us from several states away saying, 'Dad, I need help. Can I come home?' I told him, 'Of course, you know you are always welcome home, son. But you also know what the standards are in our home. And even though you're an adult, you still must respect the rules of our home. Are you ready to do that?' He said, 'Yes, I'm ready to come home.'

"Tim did well and made good on his promises while he was here. He even thanked us for raising him in a loving family.

Hard to believe those words were coming out of his mouth after all the vulgar names he had called us over the years. I wish I could say he has been reunited with his Heavenly Father. He hasn't. But we believe that will come, too. He's already taken the hard step of apologizing to us."

Extend forgiveness.
Few things cripple us like unresolved conflicts and anger from the past. Says well-known counselor and author Neil Anderson: "I have discovered in my counseling that unforgiveness is the number one avenue Satan uses to gain entrance to believers' lives. Unforgiveness is an open invitation to Satan's bondage in our lives."[3]

Forgiveness is the most difficult step toward reconciliation, especially for a wounded parent. Your forgiveness has likely been extended and abused over and over again. By now, trust has been both granted and destroyed countless times.

You may feel you have good cause for never trusting your child again, as even those positive initiatives taken by him or her will likely appear suspect or manipulative to you. Does God ask us to grant unlimited trust to a child who has proven to be untrustworthy? I don't think so. Even Jesus would not *entrust* himself to people, for he knew what was in their hearts (see Jn 2:24-25). But he did love people unconditionally, and that's what he requires of us as well (see Jn 13:34).

An essential component of unconditional love includes forgiving those who have hurt us. And God's definition of forgiveness goes far deeper than what is implied at first glance. He declares, "For I will forgive their wickedness and will remember their sins no more"(Jer 31:34). In another place he says, "As far as the east is from the west, so far has he removed our transgressions from us" (Ps 103:12).

In other words, not only does God forgive our sins, but he forgets them as well. Consider the dictionary's definition of *forget*: "to lose the remembrance of ... to treat with inattention or disregard ... to disregard intentionally; overlook; cease remembering or noticing ... to fail to become mindful at the proper time." How wonderful that we can rejoice with the apostle Paul, "Blessed is the man whose sin the Lord will never count against him" (Rom 4:8)!

Is God asking us to ignore and forget our child's past offenses and not take into consideration their destructive patterns? No, that would more closely resemble the definition of a dysfunctional enabler. Rather, as we entrust ourselves completely to God and his care, we are free to love our children and even appropriately trust them—and to do it out of genuine love. Then, even when they do let us down, we are not destroyed by it. Our ultimate identity and security rests not in our children, but in Jesus Christ. This sort of love is also the best environment for real change in our children.

Of course, forgiveness is a process for all of us, especially for those who have been wounded deeply. To expect that we are able to immediately forgive and forget is unrealistic. But when we decide that we want to forgive and begin praying to that end, real progress has already been made and we are well on our way.

Offer reconciliation.

Some people mistakenly lump forgiveness and reconciliation together, but the two are very different. Forgiveness is something we choose to do, regardless of the response of the other party. Reconciliation, on the other hand, requires a willing participation on both sides. It literally means, "to restore harmony, to bring oneself to accept." In order for reconciliation to occur several things must first be in place:

- Both parties are able to accept their own, and each other's, strengths and weaknesses.
- Both parties are willing to admit their own failures.
- Both parties desire healing for the broken relationship.
- Both parties are willing to give up their demand to be right.
- Both parties are willing to give up any desire to make the other pay.[4]

Of course, reconciliation doesn't assume that a complete transformation has taken place in our child, nor does it guarantee a change in their behavior. As always, the choice still remains with them. But our relationship will be much less conflict-centered.

Be realistic.
Parenting a wayward child often feels like one step forward and two steps back. Most of the parents I interviewed for this book saw no significant change for the better within the first year after they began applying the principles of parenting for the long haul. In many cases, things actually got worse as the family equilibrium was upset and different members subconsciously resisted such changes. But when parents remained faithful, prayerful, and consistent, significant and lasting change for the better did occur within three years in every single case.

The bottom line is this: parenting for the long haul means

that when we are already doing everything we can, we just have to keep on doing it. And wait.

Summary

When your dream for your child has died, parenting for the long haul means
- embracing the grief process
- reaching out to others
- taking steps toward reconciliation

Chapter Nine

When It's Beyond You

*If you need wisdom—if you want to know what God
wants you to do—ask him, and he will gladly tell you.*
                                                    JAMES 1:5, NLT

Jackson was covered with blood after putting his fist through
the window, yet he was silent all the way to the hospital. While
it wasn't the first time he had lost his temper and thrown a
punch, this time it had been aimed at his mother.

Like many parents of an angry teenager, Jackson's mother
had already tried a number of alternatives: counseling, youth
group, even a special camp program. But his temper and
accompanying outbursts only escalated. Was it time to have
Jackson removed from her home? If she did, would their relationship be forever doomed? Were there other possible solutions she hadn't yet thought of?

How do we decide when the issues our child is presenting
are beyond our ability to address on our own—including when
it may be necessary to remove him from home? In this chapter,
we will wade through some of those difficult waters. Such decisions are always difficult, but I hope to lay out a process whereby
one can make a well-informed, non-emotionally-charged, od-
honoring decision. One that, though painful, you can feel
confident is the best decision for your teen.

Discerning the Depth of the Problem

The first step in addressing a child's troubling behavior is to accurately assess just what type of situation you are dealing with. Most difficulties with teens fall into one of three categories: dilemmas, crises, or emergencies.

Dilemmas

When assessing the situation, first ask how long this predicament (such as criminal activity or drug use) has been going on. If you have just found out about the problem, it may feel like a crisis, but actually be a dilemma.

Joan and Steve panicked when they discovered a pack of cigarettes in their daughter's coat pocket. They mistakenly perceived the situation as a crisis rather than a dilemma, and their response—threatening to turn her over to the courts—ignited a conflict that resulted in their daughter running away from home. Their overreaction only exacerbated the problem.

Dilemmas require the least immediate response of the three. That doesn't mean the dilemma is insignificant and doesn't require attention. It means that you likely have some time to ponder, pray, and ask for advice with a cool, objective outlook before making a decision about what to do. Having the luxury of time also helps us avoid the tendency of overreacting.

Dilemmas include finding pornography on your son's computer, discovering that your son or daughter is sexually active, or realizing that your high schooler is failing three courses and may not graduate.

One good way to discern whether you are facing a dilemma

or a crisis is to ask yourself: *Can this be talked through?* If, for example, Joan and Steve had sat down with their daughter to talk through the reasons she decided to start smoking as well as some of the pros and cons of her decision, the results may have been completely different. If you can talk through the issue you're facing with your child, either on your own or with the help of a therapist, you are likely facing a dilemma.

Crises

While dilemmas can be dealt with less intensively, a crisis may require more immediate and direct action.

One example of a dilemma that has evolved into a crisis is finding out that your sexually active daughter is pregnant. It now needs your immediate attention, as your daughter is facing significant, life-changing decisions. It is critical for her to be assured immediately that you love her, support her, and will walk through this with her. Her knowing this will help her make rational decisions and give you a better platform to help her with those decisions.

When the guidance counselor informs you that your son has filed paperwork to drop out of school, the scenario has also evolved from a dilemma into a crisis. He is on the verge of making a decision that may permanently affect the rest of his life. Discovering that your son has become involved in a dangerous gang presents a crisis situation, too, as his life could be in jeopardy.

Below are some helpful questions to ask yourself in discerning how to best deal with your child's particular crisis:

- *What is the worst possible outcome of this behavior?* Begin by asking yourself, "What would happen if I did nothing at all?" From there you can begin to write down all of your options and the pros and cons of each.

- *What is my responsibility?* As much as possible, keep the responsibility on the shoulders of the person responsible for the crisis. Rather than making it an issue between you and your child, ask, "How can I best help you through this?"

- *What is my objective?* Ask yourself honestly what you are trying to accomplish. Oftentimes we take action primarily to avoid embarrassment to ourselves. Yet our ultimate goal should be the spiritual and emotional growth of our child. Consider whether or not your actions may be interfering with God's ultimate plan for your child. Always ask, "What would be in my child's best interest?"

Emergencies

Emergencies are situations that require immediate attention to avoid irreparable harm. These are "9-1-1" events.

A crisis has escalated into an emergency when you overhear your pregnant daughter making an appointment at an abortion clinic. She is about to make a decision that will forever impact her life and the life of her unborn child. An emergency is when your son's gang involvement escalates to the point where a rock is thrown through your window with a death threat note tied to it. The police now need to be brought in, and your son may need to leave your home for awhile for his safety as well as the safety of your family.

Recognizing Situations That Require Outside Intervention

Your ability to correctly assess the depth of your child's problem lies in your awareness and knowledge of the symptoms of those serious problems that may need professional attention or intervention and treatment. What follows is simply meant to point you in the right direction. If your child shows signs of any of the following problems, I would urge you to consult with a trained counselor about how best to help your child.

Anger and Violence

Anger is the dominant emotion of distressed and troubled teens, yet it is a secondary emotion. In other words, feelings of hurt, embarrassment, confusion, fear, loneliness, or insecurity are often the source of their anxiety. But because teens are usually not yet in touch with their primary emotions, all responses to stress surface as anger. And their anger has the distinct capacity to surface anger issues inside us as well.

Some children show no signs of violence at younger ages and then suddenly turn violent at home as they approach puberty. This can take a parent completely by surprise.

If your child exhibits excessive anger, there are several things you can do.

1. Come alongside your child to discover the source of the anger. Try to talk with your child about the cause of the anger. Sometimes it is long-standing issues like feeling rejected, insecure, or powerless. Having experienced physical, verbal, or sexual abuse almost always contributes tremendously to a young person's anger and rage. Other times a child's anger may come from frustrations at school. Attendance at a new school, academic struggles, or the presence of a learning disability that has gone unchecked until middle or high school are all contributing factors to anger.

As one father explains: "Jeff did very well in school until the day he entered middle school. Then, rather than having one teacher and a fairly structured environment, he had eight classes, eight teachers, eight books to lose, and barely any structure by comparison. For someone with ADD, this is a recipe for disaster. And it didn't take Jeff long to figure out that he was no longer welcome or appreciated in school. This caused a tremendous surge of anger in him, which of course he took out on his family, for he knew we were the only ones who wouldn't reject him."

If your child is struggling academically, help him or her discover areas of strength. As young people discover and experience success in their areas of giftedness, frustration and anger levels often dissipate.

If your child is feeling the brunt of bullying, you may need to speak with school officials. With the onset of adolescence, peers take on a whole new place of importance. When adolescents struggle to find an acceptable place in the peer pecking order, or are being picked on or bullied in school, they can feel a tremendous amount of internal rage. If you suspect this may be happening with your child, try to engage him or her in discussions about it in a nonthreatening way. Schools are finally beginning to take this problem seriously and are much quicker to respond than in the past.

2. Be sure your form of discipline is not demeaning your child.
Identity and respect loom large in early adolescence. If you
are using corporal punishment to discipline your adolescent,
your actions may be causing intense rage in your teen. Physical
force is a very degrading way to discipline an adolescent.

It can be challenging to find appropriate forms of discipline for teens. The command to "go to your room" often produces a face-to-face confrontation. Too many weekend
groundings can also bring on frustration and lead to alienation. Seek advice from wise, experienced parents who have
been through such struggles.

As I said earlier, you might want to discuss with your teen
what sorts of consequences would be appropriate for behavior
that you have identified as unacceptable. Such a discussion
carried out in a calmer time goes a long way toward resolving
conflict and building mutual respect and understanding.

*3. Take immediate action if your teen's violent behavior causes you
concern for his or her safety—or the safety of others.* If the onset of
violence is recent and your teen hasn't seen a counselor in the
past, you might begin with counseling. But if counseling has
been tried and failed, your child may need to be temporarily
removed from the home to deal more intensely with his or her
anger issues. Seek the counsel of others whom you trust or
who have been there. Sometimes a weekend "time out" in a
detention center can be helpful. At other times it only exacerbates the anger, especially if the source of the anger stems
from a feeling of rejection by you or your spouse.

If your teen has exhibited violence from an early age and it
has escalated to a point of danger, he may need a residential

program with its intense structure, counseling, and treatment. Long-standing anger and violence often require outside intervention.

If you discover that your child has been routinely sexually abusing younger siblings, you are required by law to report that behavior to local law enforcement officials or a social service agency. For the sake of all of your children, immediate intervention is necessary. Sexual abuse should be distinguished, however, from playful experimentation that siblings will often engage in at a young age. You may need outside counsel to help you discern the difference.

Drug and Alcohol Addiction

Alcoholism continues to be the number one drug problem in America. In fact, 93 percent of high school students report having used alcohol at some time in their lives.[1] Research indicates that as many as 10 percent of adolescents are already full-blown alcoholics.[2] Individuals who begin drinking before age fifteen are five times more likely to be alcohol dependent as adults.[3]

But it can be difficult to discern when a child may need outside treatment due to addiction. There are four categories of users:

1. *The Experimenter.* This adolescent experiments with alcohol or drugs up to four or five times in order to gain acceptance and "be in the know." Their use is short-term and low in frequency.
2. *The Recreationist.* He or she uses drugs or alcohol primarily to share pleasurable experiences with friends, not to achieve a mood or mental effect from the substance.

3. *The Seeker.* This young person deliberately seeks an altered state and uses regularly to achieve a sedative or intoxicant effect.

4. *The Addict.* Addicts cannot feel any sense of well-being or normalcy without drugs or alcohol and will do almost anything to get a "fix." They show serious deficiencies in interpersonal relationships, as they regularly choose intoxication over relationships and anything else.[4]

If you suspect your child may be addicted to drugs or alcohol, look for the presence of these other indicators:

- Withdrawal: Spends significantly more time alone in his room or another secluded place in the home. Avoids family times of interaction and fun.

- Changing relationships: Forms a new circle of friends whom she never brings home. Is secretive about names, places, and what they do together.

- Difficulties in school: Exhibits truancy, unwillingness to do homework, lack of motivation and concentration, or a sudden decline in grades.

- Resistance to authority: Is rebellious toward parents, teachers, police, and sometimes church and the youth pastor.

- Shifting interests: Shows a sudden lack of interest in grooming, neatness, or personal hygiene.

- Behavior problems: Exhibits unexplained spending, stealing, shoplifting, little regard for personal safety, frequent traffic tickets.

- Signs of depression: Displays suicidal gestures or actual attempts at suicide.

- Unusual and sustained physical complaints: Has frequent colds, flus, vomiting, constipation, abdominal distress, headaches, or tremors.
- Changes in eating habits: Has an increase or decrease in appetite, with accompanying weight gain or loss.
- Obvious signs of "being under the influence": Has alcohol on breath, slurred speech, staggering, dilated pupils, exhilaration, hallucinations, panic, or delusions.[5]

If your teen has three or more of these signs, he or she has a serious problem and needs treatment—perhaps even hospitalization, as the process of "detoxing" is most safely done under medical supervision.

The battle over drugs or alcohol is rarely won without a residential treatment program. The only other alternative for an addict is to attend thirty meetings in thirty days (such as Narcotics Anonymous or Alcoholics Anonymous) and then to remain faithful to attend weekly.[6] Most teens, however, haven't come to the necessary level of brokenness and despair required to make a commitment to attend thirty meetings in thirty days. Often, a staged intervention by friends, family, and a therapist is necessary to get an adolescent into treatment. When confronted this way, 80 percent agree to get help.[7]

The bottom line is this: addicts need help—and lots of it. For many, it is not simply a matter of discipline. Appendix A lists several resources for families struggling with a teen involved in drugs or alcohol.

Suicidal Tendencies

Suicide continues to be the second leading cause of death among teens in America. Some experts believe, however, that because many suicides are disguised as accidents, it may well be number one.[8] For every successful suicide, there are at least a hundred others who attempt it.[9]

The reasons that teens might attempt suicide include: depression, guilt, escape, family disruption, the loss of a close relationship, abuse, or as a cry for help or attention. Because teens often get wrapped up in the moment, they have difficulty seeing how things could possibly change for the better, and so many see suicide as the only way out. Teens also have difficulty understanding the long-term consequences of their behavior.

Some of the warning signs of potential suicide are listed below.

- A history of problems. Suicide is a process and rarely an impulsive act.
- Decline in performance. Grades drop, along with a decreased motivation or desire to compete.
- A recent traumatic event. Physical illness, failure in school, the breakup of a romance, or the divorce of parents may intensify already-present suicidal thoughts.
- Communication problems. Suicide may be an inarticulate cry for help by adolescents who have difficulty expressing their feelings.
- Irrational outbursts. Suicidal youth may suddenly become quick-tempered, cry easily, or become easily upset by trivial things.

- Depression. An enormous sense of sadness is almost always a warning sign.
- Change in eating or sleeping habits. Adolescents begin to sleep or eat much more or less than they usually do.
- Talk about suicide. Experts estimate that about 80 percent of persons who take their lives have talked about it with others. Some speak more verbally about it. Others may write suicidal notes or begin giving treasured objects away.
- Withdrawal. Rather than taking the initiative for new experiences, the suicidal teen may spend long hours alone in silence or listening to music.
- Despair. The suicidal teen sees the future as hopeless; the ups and downs of adolescence become mainly downs for several weeks or months.[10]

If your teen exhibits several of these signs, take it very seriously. Don't be afraid to ask, "Do you think about killing yourself?" This will communicate that you know something is wrong and open the lines of communication. If he denies it you can then say, "I just wanted to ask, because I worry and because I love you so much. If you ever do think about killing or harming yourself, please talk to me or your father first, OK?"

Also seek counsel from a mental health professional who has experience with teenagers who may struggle with depression or suicidal tendencies. In some cases, hospitalization or a long-term residential treatment facility may be necessary to get to the core of your child's struggles.

Eating Disorders

Many teenage girls struggle with eating disorders—and the number of boys is increasing as well. Reports indicate that anorexia and bulimia may impact as many as 25 percent of the adolescent population,[11] affecting a total of five to ten million girls and women and one million boys and men.[12]

Tragically, such trends are being observed in younger and younger children. A recent study found that 39 percent of girls in grades five to eight said they were on a diet. Thirteen percent of those girls said they had already binged and purged, symptoms of bulimia.[13]

To be sure, the media plays an enormous role in perpetuating this sense of insecurity that breeds eating disorders. As an example, in 1995, 3 percent of girls on the island of Fiji suffered from bulimia. That was the year television arrived. Within just three short years, the rate of bulimia among teenage girls had jumped to 17 percent.[14]

Some of the warning signs that your child may have anorexia nervosa (intentional starvation) include:

- being extremely underweight
- expressing a fear of fatness that does not subside with weight loss
- absence or suppression of menstruation
- brittle hair and nails
- decreasing ability to experience hunger, fatigue, anxiety, depression, and other sensations
- course, dry, sloughing skin

Possible warning signs of bulimia (binge eating followed by

self-induced vomiting, use of laxatives or diuretics, and extreme exercise) include:

- frequent weight fluctuations
- destructive eating patterns usually done in secret
- abdominal pain, constipation, and/or diarrhea
- muscle weakness
- irregular menstrual periods
- damage to dental enamel[15]

Teens who struggle with eating disorders almost always require outside intervention and sometimes hospitalization or long-term residential care. If you suspect your child may be suffering from an eating disorder, consult the helpful resources listed in Appendix A.

Self-Injury

One recent survey of 245 college students found that 12 percent admitted to having deliberately injured themselves.[16]

Most prevalent among girls (85 to 97 percent depending on the survey), self-injury—head banging, cutting, burning, biting, and digging at wounds—is a sign of broader problems that range from normal adolescent stress to emotional instability to severe psychiatric disorders.[17]

Self-injury can arise out of feelings of guilt, anger, self-hatred, perfectionism, cries for attention, stress, or the need to feel in control of one's body. One girl told me, "Cutting myself is the only thing that gives me relief." Others say they do it to force themselves to just "feel something."

Self-mutilation is a very complex issue. If your child shows signs of cutting, burning, biting, or digging at wounds, seek outside help or counseling. Hotlines like Rapha, Minirth-Meier Clinics, or Focus on the Family, listed in Appendix A, can refer you to appropriate places in your area.

Deciding Whether to Remove a Child From Your Home

Many of the situations listed above may require your child moving out of your home in order for him to receive the help he needs. Such a decision is always difficult, but the way it is made and how it is communicated is of utmost importance. If you have set up clear guidelines for your teen to remain in your home, and she continually disregards them, the decision to remove her should not come as a surprise.

When possible, make such a decision with the input of others, such as a counselor or well-trained pastor. At first you will likely feel a tremendous amount of guilt—not only self-induced, but sometimes from your children as well. Knowing that you have sincerely and honestly exhausted all other options and have prayerfully and wisely come to such a decision will help keep you from falling apart under the weight of self-doubt and a thousand "what ifs."

When They Must Leave

Once you realize your child needs to be removed from your home, take great care to explain to everyone in the family exactly why your son or daughter is leaving your home. Make sure everyone knows that you didn't make this decision because you "can't take it anymore" or because you're furious.

Emphasize that your child is always welcome back, but it will need to be under different circumstances. Reiterate again your love for all of your children.

When you tell your son or daughter that you have decided to remove him or her from your home, you might say something like this: "We want you here. But you know the standards that are required for all of us to live as a healthy, respectful family. I know you can live with those standards; you have for many years. But at this time, you seem unwilling. So, for the sake of you and the rest of our family, you will need to leave for a time."

As much as possible, keep the choice resting on the shoulders of your teen. He should not feel that you are rejecting him (though he may express it this way to you and others). Rather you are following through on the standards that you have clearly laid out many times.

Where Should Your Troubled Teen Go?

Your child's age will help you decide where she will go if you can no longer allow her to live at home. An eighteen-year-old is free to go anywhere. But if your child is a minor, you can't simply turn her out on the streets. She could stay with a friend's family if both you and that family agree. Better yet, you could place her in a suitable residential program where she can focus on some of those life-controlling issues that have caused her so much difficulty.

Residential treatment or hospitalization should be handled like any physical ailment requiring hospitalization. Make every effort to locate the best patient care possible. See Appendix A for a list of Christian residential programs.

Offer your child unswerving support and encouragement through the whole process. This includes participation in family counseling and a firm commitment to the necessary steps to health and wholeness for the entire family.

If the county or state is already involved with your child and has already assigned a caseworker, you might contact the caseworker about helping to remove the child. Most likely the agency has already developed a list of conditions your child must adhere to in order to stay in your home anyway. Whenever an agency is involved, communicate with the caseworker regularly, offering suggestions on the specific needs and programs that might be most helpful for your child.

After The Child Is Gone

"Parenting for the long haul" doesn't end just because your child has moved out. When handled wisely, moving out can be a significant turning point in your relationship.

Hanne and I had caught Danny using drugs a number of times while he was living with us. Each time we talked through the implications of his choices, gave appropriate consequences, and vowed to work together to see God give Danny victory in this area of his life.

With each incident would come a renewed commitment from Danny to seek God's help and power, to attend weekly support groups, and to be more honest with us. It seemed Danny really did want to change, and so we kept working with him.

Then one day we received a call from the school counselor that a student had confided in him that Danny was selling drugs to other students. We searched Danny's room and found several bags of marijuana. We then phoned his case-worker and explained the situation. The caseworker requested that we bring Danny into his office that afternoon for a "staffing"—something that was typically done once a month so Danny wouldn't suspect he was going to be placed back in lockup.

Danny was a bit puzzled by the sudden urgency of the staffing but trusted us enough to accompany us to his case-worker's office. It was there that we all informed him of the phone call that had come from the school earlier that day.

Danny was furious, claiming he had been framed by a fellow student who didn't like him, and then deceived by us, simply because we didn't want him anymore. We felt pretty lousy as we drove home. Should we have told Danny we were taking him to be locked up instead of leading him to believe otherwise? What would we do if the state wanted to place him back in our home? Was all that we had invested in him down the drain now that he was so angry with us?

We went to visit Danny a few days later in the detention center. His attitude was much different. He was very broken and repentant. He admitted to selling the drugs and promised to step up his commitment to going straight if we would just give him another chance.

We explained that we loved him deeply but that our home could not give him what he needed. We encouraged him to go through a drug treatment program, and assured him that we would continue to stay connected with him. Again, he felt rejected by us but could understand our perspective.

That was five years ago. Danny was sentenced to a drug rehab program, and was then released. He has struggled off and on since then, but we have a good relationship. He calls quite frequently, drops in at church every once in awhile, and makes every effort to be with us on holidays.

Parenting for the long haul often requires difficult choices. Don't hesitate to do what you know to be right. Assure your child of your unswerving love and commitment. Then allow time and the Lord to do what you can't.

Summary
The process of making a well-informed, non-emotionally-charged, God-honoring decision about how to best help your child includes these steps:
- discerning the depth of the problem
- recognizing situations that require outside intervention
- deciding whether to remove a child from your home

Chapter Ten

God's Agenda Is Me

"My grace is sufficient for you, for my power is made perfect in weakness." Therefore I will boast all the more gladly about my weakness, so that Christ's power may rest on me.

2 Corinthians 12:9

As Christians, we want to grow in our character and relationship with Jesus Christ. We applaud the notion of being conformed into the image of Christ (see Rom 8:29)—until we realize that this process of conforming and reshaping our character happens best, and perhaps only, in the midst of intense trial and tribulation.

For some, this process occurs within the context of personal tragedy or shattered hopes and dreams. For others, health problems may trigger the process. For me, it happened in the furnace of parenting troubled teens. And if you've read this far, it's probably safe to assume that a wayward teen is playing a significant role in how God wants to transform and reshape your life as well.

In Romans 5:1-4, the apostle Paul presents one of the richest teachings in all of Scripture. Not only does he present a concise theology of suffering, he also addresses our identity in Christ and the process whereby we become more and more Christlike in our actions.

¹Therefore, since we have been justified through faith, we have peace with God through our Lord Jesus Christ, ²through whom we have gained access by faith into this grace in which we now stand. And we rejoice in the hope of the glory of God. ³Not only so, but we also rejoice in our sufferings, because we know that suffering produces perseverance; ⁴perseverance, character; and character, hope.

ROMANS 5: 1–4

The first two verses of this chapter explain the Christian's position in Jesus Christ: We are already complete, accepted, and perfect in God's sight—that's what it means to be justified. We already have peace with God and full access to him. We already possess the fullest measure of faith, grace, and hope that we will ever possess.

Sounds great, huh? Except when we plug in the current condition of our life—which is often the polar opposite: we feel incomplete, unacceptable, and severely flawed. We feel turmoil much more often than peace. We struggle daily with a lack of faith. We feel guilty and condemned rather than grace-filled. We feel desperately hopeless, especially in light of all that we may be going through with our children.

How can these two realities—our *position* in Christ and our current *condition*—exist in such disharmony with each other? Paul states in Philippians 3:16 that we are to "live up to what we have already attained." In other words, the current condition in which we find ourselves is supposed to move us more and more toward a consistent reflection of our position as full-fledged children of God and joint heirs with Jesus.

But how? Verses 3 and 4 of Romans 5 lay out the process. But it's not pretty. It begins with the difficult words "rejoice in our sufferings."

Rejoice in Our Sufferings

Some versions of the Bible translate the term *sufferings* as "trials," "tribulations," "troubles," or "problems." But the Greek term *thlipis* literally means "pressure." It's the same word used in 2 Corinthians 1:8, in which Paul says, "We were under great *pressure, far beyond our ability to endure, so that we despaired even of life.*" Paul is describing a type of pressure that wears on you over time so that your ability to endure and stand up under it wanes, so much so that you begin to lose hope for your life.

Have you ever felt like that in the context of parenting your child? I have. I remember how I felt after a couple of years living in the discipleship home we ran for delinquent teens. I had not seen the positive changes I would have expected when someone as wonderfully capable as I poured all he had into a few needy boys. Instead of getting better, they appeared to be getting worse.

At the same time I felt trapped. I knew that God had placed me in that home, so I had no other place to go. But why was he doing this to me? It felt like he had moved me into this house only to destroy me. I told Hanne that I wished God would just take me home to heaven before I did something so awful it would disgrace his name and discredit all my life had stood for. Like Paul, I despaired of life.

What is the purpose of such pressure? Is it only to destroy us? In some ways, yes. Paul goes on to explain from his own life, "In our hearts we felt the sentence of death. But this happened that we might not rely on ourselves but on God, who raises the dead" (2 Cor 1:9).

A new day dawned for me the moment I stopped trying to figure out how I could either get out of the home we were running or get those who were causing me so much pain to move out. Instead, I began praying, *Lord, please use this home to change me. It's obvious that I'm in need of changing. I've never seen that so clearly as I do now. And I'm convinced that you've placed me here to do a deeper work in me than might otherwise have been possible; to work in me a process where I die to myself so that you can more fully live in me. I won't leave here until you're finished or until you tell me to go.*

Now I was in a place where I could embrace, rather than fight, what God wanted to do *in* me so that ultimately he could better work *through* me to minister to those around me. With that realization, I believe I took a giant step up to the second tier of this process.

Suffering Produces Perseverance

Some versions of the Bible also translate *perseverance* as "patience" or "endurance." But all miss the richness of the Greek word *hupomone*, which literally means, "to actively overcome."

The best illustration I can think of to explain this concept comes from my experience as a scuba diver. The first and most basic instruction one receives when learning to dive is to keep breathing. It sounds ridiculously simple, but to forget this can be life-threatening. Let me explain.

If you were to breathe in air at the surface, hold it, and then submerge twenty feet or so, your lungs could collapse. That's because the pressure at the surface is much less than the pressure in water twenty feet deep. In the same way, if you breathe in air at twenty feet below the water's surface and hold your breath until you came to the surface, your lungs could explode because pressure around you becomes less and less and the air in your lungs expands to equalize. A scuba regulator equalizes the pressure of the air you breathe from your tank to match the pressure in the water around you, but it doesn't help if you don't keep breathing.

What's the spiritual lesson here? It's this: We need God's overcoming power within us to equal the pressure being applied upon us from outside forces. We can't rely upon yesterday's experience with God or we'll collapse. God's plan is not always to remove the outside pressures, but rather to fill us with his overcoming power and strength.

The apostle Paul explains it in a profound way in 2 Corinthians 4:8-9: "We are hard pressed on every side, but not crushed; perplexed, but not in despair; persecuted, but not abandoned; struck down, but not destroyed."

Perseverance Produces Character

The Greek word for *character* is *dokime*, which literally means "sterling silver." It is descriptive of the process whereby metal is put through a refining fire so that all of its impurities are melted away.

Many of us view Christian maturity as a process of training our old flesh to become better and better. Yet the Bible teaches that we are to crucify our old fleshly nature and begin living in the power of the new nature that we possess as new creations in Christ (2 Cor 5:17, Gal 2:20). This is the image contained in the word *character.*

The development of character is not about training our flesh or even about getting "more" of Christ. We possess all of him that we will ever have at the moment of our conversion. Rather, it is a process of burning away our old nature, refining us so that what remains is a more pure display of the nature of Christ. Job's words convey the concept well: "When He has tried me, I will come forth as refined gold" (Jb 23:10, AMPLIFIED).

There's nothing like a wayward child to reveal one's dire need for such a process. Before parenting troubled teens, I had always seen myself as a rather good and gracious person. But in our home, the place where I most wanted to extend grace, there was none to be found. Instead, anger ruled my most prized and precious relationships. Part of my problem was a very inadequate definition of grace. I had assumed that grace meant being nice, cordial, not particularly prone to anger. But the Bible defines *charis*, the Greek word for grace, altogether differently. It is "the divine influence upon the heart, and its reflection in the life."[1]

In other words, grace is a completely *un*human commodity! It's a "God thing." The only time grace will truly be displayed in our lives is when it is adequately reflected from God himself. Unfortunately, I'm not a particularly good reflector. But God's refining process, allowing suffering to produce perseverance, which in turn produces character, is where I've experienced the greatest display of his amazing grace. I've also discovered that I need to receive a bucket full in order to dispense a teaspoon to somebody else. Yet I am convinced that those occasional teaspoons of grace have made the real difference in the lives of those I have been called to serve.

Quite often God develops our character at those times when we least recognize it—often at the very times when we feel most like a failure. But little by little, we realize that we are a completely different person because of what we experienced during those times.

I love getting together with Don and Bev and hearing them speak through their pain and deep love of their son Ricky. "We are still trying to figure out what good will come of all this," says Bev. "I say to God over and over, 'OK, Lord, I get the picture. Patience. Perseverance. Trust. I get it. But he's twenty-four years old now. How long, Lord?'" She can't see how much good has come out of this, but it's so obvious to me every time I meet with them.

Don is a black-and-white type of guy. He is not naturally compassionate toward those who can't produce or make the cut. But after parenting Ricky, he says, "I've become much more comfortable in the 'grays.'" And his heart has become much softer as well. "The other night I was walking with a friend in Chicago and saw a group of rough, intimidating-looking kids on the streets. In the past, I might have felt a little fearful or thought to myself, 'thugs.' But now I look at them and think, 'These kids are someone's children,' and I say a prayer for them."

Don is even mentoring a seventh grade boy from church

who exhibits many of the same struggles that his own son had at that age. What would make Don into such a compassionate individual? Consider the very meaning of the term *compassion*. It's derived from the Latin words *com* and *pati,* which literally translated means "with pain."

Similarly, Bev says, "When I heard the news of the school shootings at Columbine High School, my first response was to pray and weep for the parents of Eric Harris and Dylan Klebold. And I have prayed for them so often since then, knowing how easily we could have been such parents. We searched our son's room regularly, yet never knew he had a .357 magnum until one time he was arrested and the police found it on him. Although we suspected Ricky did drugs, we found no evidence until he had to be hospitalized because of an overdose."

When I think of people who possess real character, Don and Bev are among the first who come to my mind. God has used their pain to form them into compassionate and caring servants of his.

Character Produces Hope

Hope. It is defined in so many different ways: "to wish for something with great expectation," "to desire or long for," "to expect or anticipate." But the biblical definition of *hope* (*elpis*) is not about wishing or even believing that things will ultimately turn out as we desire. Rather, it is the confident assurance that God will use our circumstances to produce much-needed change. Yes, it's about the changes he is producing in us as parents, but it is also the assurance that God is working overtime in our children's lives.

Ron explains the hope he has for his son, Justin, this way: "What keeps me going is that it's not over till it's over. When I listen to the testimonies of people who have been rebellious, addicted, in jail, and without hope, I immediately think, *Someone had to parent these prodigals during their rebellious years. I wonder what the Lord is going to do with our son's life?*"

His wife Jean says, "Most parents hope that their children grow up to be well-adjusted adults who make positive choices. My hope has changed over the years. I hope that God will use this difficult path he has placed us on to make a difference in someone else's life. There is a whole generation of kids growing up who can relate to Justin, and who might only listen to someone like him. Justin is learning disabled and chemically-dependent. He has ADD and has been in gangs and is a convicted criminal. Maybe the fact that he struggled for so long before getting his life together will someday encourage others like him to realize that there is hope for them as well. I know, too, that a lot of parents can relate to what we've gone through and could use friends like us."

Jean's definition of hope matches closely the one Paul gives in 2 Corinthians 1:3-7:

> Praise be to the God and Father of our Lord Jesus Christ, the Father of compassion and the God of all comfort, who comforts us in all our troubles, so that we can comfort those in any trouble with the comfort we ourselves have received from God. For just as the sufferings of Christ flow over into our lives, so also through Christ our

comfort overflows. If we are distressed, it is for your comfort and salvation; if we are comforted, it is for your comfort, which produces in you patient endurance of the same sufferings we suffer. And our *hope* for you is firm, because we know that just as you share in our sufferings, so also you share in our comfort (emphasis added).

A Better Understanding of Our Heavenly Father

The experience of raising a rebellious child gives parents a unique insight into the heart and character of God. It's easy to forget that the pain of a prodigal's parent, as portrayed in the fifteenth chapter of Luke, is first about the heart of God, a heart that aches for his own children.

When I was in the midst of my deepest struggles with the teens in our home, I began meditating on the fact that God never withholds his love and blessing from us, even though he can see the future and knows that we may fail miserably and disgrace his name. That blew me away. I had always been willing to invest in any kid—as long as he or she proved to be a worthwhile investment. But when it looked as if he might be going down the drain, I quickly cut my emotional ties so that I wouldn't go down with him.

I started thinking about the way Jesus loved people like Judas Iscariot. It's clear from Scripture that Jesus knew Judas would betray him. Yet he never withheld his love from him. He even entrusted him to be treasurer! The thirteenth chapter of John beautifully illustrates how Jesus showed Judas the fullest extent of his love by feeding and washing his feet, even moments before Judas would betray him.

I knew that I didn't love like that, but I was also convinced that anything short of Jesus' kind of love was not *really* love at all. Instead, it was merely making a wise investment of my time and energies and loving only those who could appropriately reciprocate. Of such actions Jesus said, "Do not even pagans do that?" (Mt 5:47).

I began asking God, "How do *you* handle rebellious kids?" And then more pertinently, "How do you handle me? What keeps you from just giving up on *me?*"

I found myself drawn to the story of the Prodigal Son. I had always felt a little uncomfortable with that story. It didn't seem like very responsible parenting to me. After all, how was this kid to learn his lesson if his father so easily took him back? But I had always read this parable through the eyes of the self-righteous older brother. Now I was seeing myself not as the older brother, but as the younger one. And for the first time, feeling grateful for the father's response.

As I interviewed scores of parents for this book, I realized that I wasn't the only one coming to such an awakening. In fact, almost without exception, those parents who had successfully undergone the painful process of seeing their struggles develop perseverance, character, and hope all told me they were deeply influenced by this parable.

"Through parenting Jason, I've come to realize more and more just how much of a prodigal I am, and of my need to receive grace upon grace every day," explained one father. "If I'm in this state with my Heavenly Father, how can I not offer grace to my earthly son? When I read the story of the Prodigal Son I don't see primarily 'tough love.' I see grace. And when

I came to realize that, it completely changed how I related to my own rebellious son."

What About You?

Several years ago I was bold enough to pray, *Father, conform me into the image of your Son.* Looking back, I realize that God has used my experiences of parenting troubled kids, more than anything else, to answer that prayer. Because of them, I am not the same person I was ten years ago. I am not even the same as I was one year ago.

Can you embrace such a prayer and the corresponding gift of your son or daughter that God has entrusted to you? Take a moment now to thank him for your child and for the deeper work he wants to do in you as well. Then fall humbly at his feet, asking for the moment-by-moment wisdom and strength needed to be the parent he has called you to be—for the long haul.

Appendix A

Resource Directory of Services for Parents

Support Groups For Parents

1. *Relief for Hurting Parents* Support Groups
Based on the book *Relief for Hurting Parents* by Buddy Scott.
Exist throughout the United States. Contact them to start
or attend a support group.
979-297-5700
P.O. Box 804
Lake Jackson, TX 77566
www.buddyscott.com

2. *You're Not Alone* Conferences
Hosted annually in various parts of the United States for
ministers and others whose children are hooked on drugs
or alcohol. Their website also contains helpful answers to
many of the questions parents of abusers ask themselves.
480-752-8994
PMB Suite 103
10105 East Via Linda
Scottsdale, AZ 85258
www.notalone.org

3. *Turning Point Ministries*
Helps churches start support groups for people with addictions and eating disorders. Groups for parents and teens meet throughout North America.
1-800-879-4770
P.O. Box 22127
Chattanooga, TN 37422-2127
info@turningpointministries.org
www.turningpointministries.org

Support Groups for Teens Struggling With Alcohol or Drug Addiction

1. *Overcomers Outreach* support groups
A nationwide Christian 12-step support group for individuals and families. Overcomers Outreach provides a two-way bridge between traditional 12-step support groups and people within churches of all denominations.
1-800-310-3001
P.O. Box 2208
Oakhurst, CA 93644
www.overcomersoutreach.org

2. *Alcoholics Anonymous*
Provides helpful information on dealing with alcoholism. Find out about meeting days and times at AA's website.
1-800-509-2415
P.O. Box 459
Grand Central Station
New York, NY 10163
www.alcoholics-anonymous.org

3. Al-Anon/Alateen

Al-Anon is a support group for those who live with the problem drinking of a relative or friend. Alateen is a 12-step recovery program for teens and is part of the Al-Anon Family Groups.
1-888-4ALANON
1600 Corporate Landing Parkway
Virginia Beach, VA 23454-5617
www.WSO@al-anon.org

Help Lines

1. *Focus on the Family*

This hotline will help connect you with specialized ministries across the country.
1-800-A-FAMILY (232-6459)
www.family.org

2. *The Minirth Clinic*

1-888-MINIRTH (646-4784)
2100 North Collins Blvd., Suite 200
Richardson, TX 75080
www.christiancounselor.com

3. *Rapha*

Christ-centered care for Christians in need of help.
1-800-383-4673
www.raphacare.com

4. *American Society of Addiction Medicine*
Gives a list of programs as well as a discussion of approaches
for various addictions.
301-656-3920
4601 North Park Ave., Arcade Suite 101
Chevy Chase, MD 20815
www.asam.org

5. *Center for Disease Control and Prevention*
National AIDS Hotline, 1-800-342-2437
National HIV/AIDS hotline (Spanish), 1-800-344-7532
National STD hotline, 1-800-227-8922
1600 Clifton Road
Atlanta, GA 30333
www.cdc.gov

6. *National Runaway Switchboard*
Twenty-four-hour helpline for teens and parents.
1-800-621-4000
3080 N. Lincoln Ave.
Chicago, IL 60657

7. *National Center for Missing & Exploited Children*
1-800-843-5678
Charles B. Wang International Children's Building
699 Prince Street
Alexandria, VA 22314-3175
www.missingkids.com

8. *Youth Crisis Hotline*
1-800-448-4663

9. *National Drug Abuse Hotline*
1-800-662-4357

Written Resources

1. *Straight Ahead Ministries*
Books and materials designed for troubled teens and those who minister to them.
508-616-9286
P.O. Box 1011
Westborough, MA 01581
info@straightahead.org
www.straightahead.org

2. *R.A. "Buddy" Scott/Allon Publishing*
Christian books for parents and struggling teens.
979-297-5700
www.buddyscott.com

3. *The Will Rogers Institute*
Free booklets on the effects, composition, motives, treatment, and consequences of psychoactive drugs.
914-761-5550
785 Mamaroneck Ave.
White Plains, NY 10605

4. *Centers for Disease Control and Prevention*
A variety of publications and software pertaining to youth health issues.
www.cdc.gov/publications

5. *Turning Point Ministries*
Materials and training conferences on Biblical approaches to life-controlling problems.
1-800-879-4770
P.O. Box 22127
Chattanooga, TN 37422-2127
info@turningpointministries.org
www.turningpointministries.org

6. *Self-Help Sourcebook*
Comprehensive online listing of support groups for alcoholics and their families.
614-764-0143
570 Metro Place
Dublin, OH 43017
www.mentalhelp.net

7. *National Institute of Drug Abuse*
301-443-1124
National Institutes of Health
6001 Executive Blvd., Room 5213
Bethesda, MD 20892
www.nida.gov

8. *National Institute on Alcohol Abuse and Alcoholism*
Website for answers to questions such as how to tell if you're an alcoholic.
www.niaaa.nih.gov

Residential Programs

1. *Rapha*
Residential treatment facilities throughout United States for addictions and eating disorders.
1-800-227-2657
www.raphacare.com

2. *Remuda Ranch*
Christian treatment center specializing in treating eating disorders.
1-800-445-1900
www.remuda-ranch.com

3. *The Fold*
Christian residential program offering hope and healing for troubled teens and families in crisis.
802-626-5620
P.O. Box 1188
Lyndonville, VT 05843

4. *Fields of Harvest*
Christian residential program for emotionally troubled teens.
802-635-7807
1296 Collins Hill Road
Johnston, VT 05656
www.fieldsofharvestvt.org

5. *Alpha Academy*
Residential programs for males needing structure and direction.
1-877-LIFEMAP
P.O. Box 13958
San Luis Obispo, CA 93406
www.lifemap.net

6. *Eckerd Family Youth Alternatives, Inc.*
Wilderness camping programs for teens and preteens with behavioral problems at home and school.
1-800-554-4357
100 N. Starcrest Drive
P.O. Box 7450
Clearwater, FL 33758-7450
www.eckerd.org

7. *Teen Challenge International*
Christian drug and alcohol rehabilitation centers throughout U.S. for men and women 18 and older. Some programs may accept teens.
417-862-6969
3728 W. Chestnut Expressway
Springfield, MO 65802
www.teenchallenge.com

8. *His Mansion Ministries*
Christian residential program for men and women over 18.
603-464-5555
P.O. Box 40
Hillsboro, NH 03244
www.hismansion.org

9. *Boys Village*
For boys 11-18 struggling with drug, alcohol, and sexual problems.
330-264-3232
P.O. Box 518
Smithville, Ohio 44677
www.boys-village.com

10. *Victory Outreach International*
Christian drug, alcohol, and gang rehabilitation program, especially for Hispanic youth.
626-961-4910
P.O. Box 3490
San Dimas, CA 91773-4437
info@victoryoutreach.org

11. *Glenhaven Youth Ranch*
Christian residential program for at risk boys.
501-432-5339
HC-68, Box 709
Plainview, AR 72857
glenhaven@glenhavenyouthranch.org

12. *SunHawk Academy, Inc.*
Wilderness-oriented residential program for troubled youth and their families.
1-800-214-3878
948 N. 1300 West
St. George, UT 84770
info@sunhawk.org

13. *Adolescent Services International*
Directory designed to assist parents, providers, and health care professionals in finding the best environment for the special needs of teens in crisis.
www.defiantteen.com

Learning Style Preference Assessment

Nine Ways to Be Smart
Assessment for Children and Adults
© *Dell Coats Erwin*

This simple assessment was developed by Dell Coats Erwin based on the work of Dr. Howard Gardner. He calls this model of intelligence the "multiple intelligences," called by others "learning styles and preferences."

Everyone has some degree of intelligence in all nine areas, but most people are stronger in one or more. Knowing where you are strong can help you understand yourself better and learn better. Knowing where you are not strong can show you areas to work on. As you learn and grow, you will become stronger in each area.

Schools are becoming more and more aware of nontraditional learning styles. Knowing the results of this assessment can help parents discuss their children's educational needs with teachers and school administrators.

Name:_____

Put a check beside each statement that is true about you or your child.

1. Word Smart – *Linguistic Intelligence*

____ I enjoy word games, puns, and rhymes.

____ I keep a journal.

____ I like to read and do it a lot.

____ I write, speak, or teach regularly.

____ I enjoy explaining ideas to others.

____ I like word games like Scrabble or Anagrams.

____ I often contact friends through notes and letters.

____ I have a good memory for names, places, dates, and other information.

2. Thinking-Numbers Smart – *Logical-Mathematical Intelligence*

____ I have figured out how long it takes to get home from work or church.

____ I enjoy puzzles and solving problems.

____ I can analyze numbers quickly.

____ I can do math in my head.

____ I like chess and/or checkers.

____ I keep things neat and orderly.

____ I like step-by-step directions.

____ Math and/or science are/were favorite subjects.

3. Picture Smart – *Spatial Intelligence*

____ I daydream a lot.

____ I am interested in colors and patterns.

____ I enjoy tinkering with things.

____ I am good with giving and reading directions.

____ I prefer reading material that is heavily illustrated.

____ I enjoy jigsaw puzzles, mazes, and Lego blocks.

____ I have vivid dreams at night.

____ I like to draw, doodle, and create art.

4. Music Smart – *Musical Intelligence*

____ I often sing, hum, or whistle songs to myself.

____ I tap out rhythms and/or sing when listening to music.

____ I love to go to concerts.

____ I play a musical instrument, or am a vocalist, or sing in a choir.

____ I hear sounds others miss—bells ringing far away, birds, or crickets chirping.

____ I like to have music playing all the time.

____ I find it hard to concentrate while listening to the radio or TV.

____ I like musicals better than dramatic plays.

5. Body Smart – *Bodily Kinesthetic Intelligence*

____ I can mimic other people's movements and behaviors.

____ I enjoy taking part in sports and/or physical activities; i.e. swimming, hiking, or skating.

____ I like either dancing, acting, aerobics, martial arts, or miming.

____ I move a lot when sitting on a chair.

____ I am good in woodworking, sewing, carving, or model building.

____ I need to touch things to learn more about them.

____ I find it hard to sit still for long periods.

____ I use a lot of gestures or other body language when I talk to someone.

6. People Smart – *Interpersonal Intelligence*

____ I am aware of others' feelings and care a lot about them.

____ I like to make new friends and am comfortable around new people.

____ People come to me for advice.

____ I am seen as a leader and/or teach or manage others.

____ I have at least three close friends.

____ I consider myself a leader (or others have called me that).

____ I enjoy group games and group activities.

____ I learn best when working with others.

7. Self Smart – *Intrapersonal Intelligence*

____ I can have fun alone.

____ I enjoy either meditation, prayer, or thinking alone.

____ I keep a journal that includes inner thoughts.

____ I consider myself to be strong-willed or independent minded.

____ I am deeply aware of my inner feelings and thoughts.

____ I like to work on projects alone.

____ I have self-confidence.

____ I often spend time alone thinking about important life questions.

8. Nature Smart – *Naturalist Intelligence*

____ I enjoy animals and/or have a pet.

____ I enjoy growing plants and know the names of many.

____ I often notice plants and animals wherever I go.

____ When outside, I closely notice the sky, clouds, and plants.

____ I like collecting rocks and seashells.

____ I enjoy going to the beach or walking in the woods.

____ I like to watch fish in an aquarium for a long time.

____ I care very much about the environment and endangered species.

9. Deep-Meanings Smart – *Existentialism Intelligence*

____ I enjoy reading or listening to information about the meaning of life.

____ I often ask questions that begin with "Why?" and "How?"

____ I like to daydream about why things happen as they do.

____ I wonder a lot about why people were born and why they die.

____ I think a lot about God and heaven.

____ I like to read the Bible and other religious books.

____ I like to listen to sermons and talks about deep subjects.

____ I pray a lot in a way that involves talking to and listening to God.

Totals for All Nine Ways of Being Smart

____ Linguistic intelligence (word smart)

____ Logical-Mathematical intelligence (thinking-numbers smart)

____ Spatial intelligence (picture smart)

____ Musical intelligence (music smart)

____ Bodily-kinesthetic intelligence (body smart)

____ Interpersonal intelligence (people smart)

____ Intrapersonal intelligence (self smart)

____ Naturalist intelligence (nature smart)

____ Existentialism intelligence (deep-meanings smart)

Meaning of Scores

This is not a test. You cannot make a good or a bad score. The scores are not like grades. You will be high in some and low in some. The ones you are highest in indicate the style that you learn best with.

The scores will help you know yourself better. They may also help others understand you better. If you are a young person, these scores can help parents and teachers know you better and help you do better with schoolwork.

NOTE: This simple assessment is not comprehensive and only provides clues regarding strengths in each intelligence area. In fact, one weakness of the assessment is that it is conducted mainly through the linguistic intelligence. The best way to assess the intelligences may be through observation of performance and activities based on each intelligence.

For more complete assessments visit the following websites:

www.thomasarmstrong.com
www.applest.com/profile.htm>www.applest.com/profile.htm
for an assessment that can be completed online from Cynthia Tobias
www.learningstyle.com (Information on learning styles from Price, a link from Dr. Dunn. For $5 the company will score an assessment.)
www.KaganOnline.com for many other products on unique learning styles

About the Author

Scott Larson, D.Min., founded Straight Ahead Ministries with his wife Hanne in 1987. Straight Ahead is a national ministry focused on reaching juvenile offenders. Scott and Hanne have also lived for nine years in a discipleship home for teens released from juvenile jails. Scott has written four other books on ministering to troubled teens and is a popular speaker for youth and adults. He can be reached at slarson@straightahead.org or by writing Straight Ahead Ministries, P.O. Box 1011, Westboro, MA 01532. Other materials on ministering to troubled teens can be accessed through the website www.straightahead.org.

Contributor Peter Vanacore, MSW, LICSW, is National Field Director for Straight Ahead Ministries. Peter has counseled countless troubled teens and their parents for more than twenty years and lives with his wife and three children in Westborough, Massachusetts. He can be reached at pvanacore@straightahead.org.

Notes

Chapter Two
Common Myths Parents Hold About Their Kids

1. John White, *Parents In Pain* (Downers Grove, Ill.: InterVarsity Press, 1979), 43.
2. Merrill F. Unger, *Unger's Bible Dictionary Third Edition* (Chicago: Moody Press, 1966), 896.
3. Cynthia Ulrich Tobias, *You Can't Make Me!* (Colorado Springs, Colo.: WaterBrook, 1999), 11.
4. *Tell Me the Facts about Learning Disabilities,* National Institute of Mental Health, www.ldonline.org/ccldinfo.
5. *Overview of Learning Disabilities,* National Institue of Mental Health (1993), NIH Publication No. 93-3611.
6. David G. Fassler and Lynne S. Dumas, *Help Me, I'm Sad: Recognizing, Treating, and Preventing Childhood and Adolescent Depression* (Middlesex, England: Penguin Books, 1997), 2; and James Garbarino, *Lost Boys: Why Our Sons Turn Violent and How We Can Save Them* (New York: The Free Press, 1999), 41.
7. Foster W. Cline and Jim Fay, *Parenting Teens with Love & Logic: Preparing Adolescents for Responsible Adulthood* (Colorado Springs, Colo.: Piñon, 1992), 111.
8. Eugene Peterson, *Like Dew Your Youth: Growing Up with Your Teenager* (Grand Rapids, Mich.: Eerdmans, 1994), 27.
9. Shannon Brownlee, "Inside the Teen Brain" *U.S. News & World Report,* August 9, 1999, 46-47.

Three
Common Myths Parents Hold About Parenting

1. Wendy Murray Zoba, "The Missing Mother," *Christianity Today*, October 26, 1998, 78.
2. John White, *The Fight* (Downers Grove, Ill.: InterVarsity Press, 1976), 219.
3. Adapted from H. Norman Wright, *Loving a Prodigal: A Survival Guide for Parents of Rebellious Children* (Colorado Springs, Colo.: Chariot Victor, 1999), 17.
4. Adapted from Laurie Hall, *The Cleavers Don't Live Here Anymore* (Ann Arbor, Mich.: Servant, 2000), 21.
5. Jack and Judith Balswick, *The Family: A Christian Perspective on the Contemporary Home* (Grand Rapids, Mich.: Baker, 1991), 133.
6. Nielson, Linda. *Adolescence: A Contemporary View, 3rd Edition* (Fort Worth, Tex.: Harcourt Brace College Publishers, 1996), 350-51.

Chapter Four
Protecting Your Marriage and Family

1. Adapted from Ann Kaiser, *Living Through a Personal Crisis* (New York: Ballantine, 1984), 66-67.
2. Adapted from Marilyn McGinnis, *Parenting Without Guilt* (San Bernadino, Calif.: Here's Life, 1987), 97-100.

Chapter Five
Strategies for Your Own Survival

1. Kevin Huggins, *Parenting Adolescents* (Colorado Springs, Colo.: Nav Press, 1989), 150.
2. Thomas à Kempis, *Imitation of Christ* (London: Penguin Books, 1954), 132.

Chapter Six
What Your Child Needs Most

1. Steven S. Hall, "The Bully in the Mirror," *The New York Times Magazine*, August 22, 1999, 35.
2. "Turning Points: Preparing American Youth for the Twenty-first Century," (1989), The Carnegie Council on Adolescent Development, as cited in Patricia Hersch, *A Tribe Apart*, (New York: Fawcett Columbine, 1998), 12.
3. Adapted from Cline and Fay, 146.
4. Adapted from Bob George, *Growing in Grace* (Eugene, Ore.: Harvest, 1991), 175-76.
5. Adapted from Margie M. Lewis with Gregg Lewis, *The Hurting Parent* (Grand Rapids, Mich.: Zondervan, 1988), 73-74.
6. Survey cited by Guy Doud in a general session at *Youth Specialties National Youth Workers Convention* in Chicago, 1988.
7. Don and Katie Fortune, *Discover Your Children's Gifts* (Grand Rapids, Mich.: Chosen, 1993).
8. Adapted from Cline and Fay, 225-26.

9. "National Early Teen Survey" conducted in 1998 by KidsPeace, Inc. of Orefield, Pa.
10. Survey conducted by Barna Research Group, cited in "Who Influences Teens?" *AFA Journal,* September 1998, 8.

Chapter Seven
Keeping a Spark of Faith Alive

1. Beth Moore, *Breaking Free: Making Liberty in Christ a Reality in Life* (Nashville, Tenn.: LifeWay, 1999), 160.
2. White, 93,165. *The Fight* (Downers Grove, Ill.: InterVarsity Press, 1976), 93, 165.

Chapter Eight
The Death of a Dream

1. Wright, 12.
2. Descriptions of these four stages adapted from material presented in Wright, 23-36.
3. Neil T. Anderson, *Victory over the Darkness: Realizing the Power of Your Identity in Christ* (Ventura, Calif.: Regal, 1990), 201.
4. Adapted from David Stoop and James Masteller, *Forgiving Our Parents, Forgiving Ourselves* (Ann Arbor, Mich.: Servant, 1991), 264-67.

Chapter Nine
When It's Beyond You

1. G. Beschner, "Understanding Teenage Drug Use," in *Teen Drug Use*, ed. G. Beschner and S. Friedman (Lexington, Mass.: Health, 1986).

2. Susan Brink, "When Being First Isn't Best," *U.S. News & World Report*, May 7, 2001, 54.

3. Jeffrey Kluger, "How to Manage Teen Drinking," *Time*, June 18, 2001, 44.

4. Adapted from Les Parrott III, *Helping the Struggling Adolescent: A Guide to Thirty Common Problems for Parents, Counselors & Youth Workers* (Grand Rapids, Mich.: Zondervan, 1993), 95-96.

5. Adapted from Rich Van Pelt, *Intensive Care: Helping Teenagers in Crisis* (Grand Rapids, Mich.: Zondervan, 1988), 190-91.

6. Adapted from R. A. Buddy Scott, *Relief for Hurting Parents: What to Do and How to Think When You're Having Trouble with Your Kids* (Nashville, Tenn.: Oliver Nelson, 1989), 220.

7. Susan Brink, "How to Help an Alcoholic," *U.S. News & World Report*, May 7, 2001, 56.

8. Parrott, 308.

9. I.B. Weiner, "Psychopathology in Adolescence," in *Handbook of Adolescent Psychology*, ed. J. Adelson (New York: Wiley, 1980).

10. Adapted from Parrott, 309.

11. M.J. Maloney and W.M. Klykylo, "An Overview of Anorexia Nervosa, Bulimia, and Obesity in Children and Adolescents," *Journal of the American Academy of Child Psychiatry* 22 (1983): 99-107.

12. "How Do You See Yourself? Addressing Anorexia and Bulimia," Turning Point Ministries brochure, Chattanooga, Tenn., 2000.

13. Barbara Kantrowitz and Pat Wingert, "The Truth about Tweens," *Newsweek*, October 18, 1999, 69.

14. *Newsweek*, May 31, 1999, 70.

15. "How Do You See Yourself? Addressing Anorexia and Bulimia."

16. K. Conterio and W. Lader, *Bodily Harm: The Breakthrough Healing Program for Self-Injurers* (New York: Hyperion, 1998), 46.

17. Polly Nichols, "Bad Body Fever and Deliberate Self-Injury," *Reclaiming Children and Youth*, Fall 2000, 152.

Chapter Ten
God's Agenda Is Me

1. James Strong, "Greek Dictionary of the New Testament," *Strong's Exhaustive Concordance* (Gordonsville, Tenn.: Dugan), 77.